CW00972113

PEOPLE
LIKE US

*A Season Among
the Upper Classes*

Charles Jennings

LITTLE, BROWN AND COMPANY

A *Little, Brown* Book

First published in Great Britain by
Little, Brown and Company 1997

A CIP catalogue record for this book
is available from the British Library.

ISBN 0 316 64003 4

Typeset in Bembo by M Rules
Printed and bound in Great Britain by
Clays Ltd, St Ives plc

Little, Brown and Company (UK)
Brettenham House
Lancaster Place
London WC2E 7EN

ACKNOWLEDGEMENTS

With thanks to Melanie Cable-Alexander, Jane Charteris, Jamie Douglas-Home, Joanna Halliday, Christopher Hirst, Anna MacLeod, Jamie Douglas McDonald-Smith, Dr Tim Palmer, Dr Tim Reilly, Caroline Steane, Alex Stitt, John and Katharine Verill, and Caroline Warburton.

Thanks also to Richard Beswick, who always has my best ideas.

ONE

I was at a wedding reception in the grounds of a vast eighteenth-century stately home in Dorset. I was the only person there not wearing a morning suit. I felt like a beetle in a hairdresser's. We all sat in a marquee as big as a hangar and ate. The woman on my left wore a bottle-green dress and said she'd been at school with Princess Diana.

'Diana's terribly vengeful,' said the woman in green. 'Quite mad. She's dropped all her old schoolfriends, you know. All of them. She only hangs around with lefty people now.'

I pursed my lips and nodded, as if I knew what she was talking about. Then she went on, 'Of course, at the *Sun*, you know, they've got this Pandora's Box of pictures of the royal family.'

Meaning?

'Well, there's one of Fergie and a glass-topped coffee table. I mean, everyone *knows*.'

Just then a bizarre man with oiled hair, an orchid in the

buttonhole of his tailcoat and a breathtakingly camp manner drew up alongside the woman in green. He held a cigarette in his cocked hand and sounded like Brian Sewell.

'Where's my wife?' he cried.

We all looked round. A frowzy blonde in chocolate velvet was staggering about on the far side of the marquee.

'Oh, she's buggered orf,' said the man with oiled hair, gesturing with his cig towards the frowzy blonde. 'The way they do! Just buggered orf!'

'Toby,' said the woman who'd been at school with Diana, 'you're being outrageous.'

'Oh, darling! I love being outrageous! I mean, what else is life for?'

To my right, two youngish women were behaving unbelievably. They were completely drunk and shouting their heads off. One dragged a bespectacled man on to her lap while the other tried to pull his trousers down. He managed to fight them off, but then they were joined by an even drunker woman. The three hoydens fell on the ground in front of the official wedding photographer, screaming, 'We're the Three Beauties! We're the Three Beauties! Photograph *us*!'

A man in a funeral director's frock coat edged in black satin turned and said to me, in a vaguely accusing manner, 'Do you *know* these people?'

I said I didn't, and asked him why he was dressed as a funeral director at a wedding.

'That's my Eton pop tailcoat,' he said with a frozen smile. 'Still fits me, you see.'

The woman in green gripped my arm. She was the Old Etonian's wife. She was drunk, too. 'You don't want to worry about Roddy,' she said helpfully. 'It's his age. He gets terribly crusty. The thing is' – she leaned towards me, her large pink eyes

focusing hard – 'when you're over thirty, the sex disappears completely. You're too tired, if you're a man, you see. Something to do
with having to go to the lavatory all the time in the middle of the
night. Roddy has to go twice a night. How often do you have to
go?'

I don't know what it is about posh people. I don't know why the
British should bother to have the only large-scale monarchy still
extant in Europe, with all the fawnings and obsessions that entails.
I don't know how it is that even Barbara Cartland could say, after
jockey Frankie Dettori had come close to snogging the Queen in
his elation at winning the Ribblesdale Stakes on her horse, 'The
Queen is sacred, above ordinary people, and shouldn't be kissed.'
Nor do I understand why we still formally recognise the aristocracy as being different from the rest of us. And I don't know why
we're so morbidly neurotic about where we come from and what
social relationship we bear to the person we're standing next to.
(Yob? Toff? Bourgeois dullard?)
   It does seem to have been this way for a depressingly long time,
though. The French writer and traveller Jean Rouquet observed
in 1755 that 'the Englishman always has in his hands an accurate
pair of scales in which he scrupulously weights up the birth, the
rank, and . . . the wealth of the people he meets, in order to adjust
his behaviour towards them accordingly'. Nearly 250 years go by
and we still do it. Why? What's the matter with us?
   In my case, class-consciousness was something that crept up on
me in my teens, like sexual awareness. Born into the North
London suburbs, I spent about eighteen years believing that
everyone else in the world lived like me. Some people obviously
had more money, since their fathers would drop them off at my
banal (but fee-paying) school in glistening Mercedes–Benzes and
Jaguars, while their mothers would pick them up in Jensens. I was

---

being ferried around in a Ford Cortina at the time. Conversely, some people used to go to different schools, crop their hair, call us names, beat the crap out of us on the Tube and steal our fares. Yet I assumed that these people all came from suburban villas identical to mine; had suburban *lives* identical to mine.

It was only after I had tricked my way into Oxford University that I realised the situation was more complicated than that. About the third thing I did after arriving, sweating with nerves, as a fresher in college, was to spot a new boy who'd been photographed in the society pages of *Vogue*. Blinded by the need to make some sort of human contact, I marched over to him and said, 'Hi! Weren't you in *Vogue*?' He looked at me as if I'd just farted up his jacket and said, 'Yes.' Then he simply turned his back on me. Etonian, it transpired. *Debrett's Peerage*. You never met these people in Finchley.

I then spent three years learning that, to my amazement and horror, there was not just one life being led at Oxford which had nothing to do with suburban North London: there were hundreds. I found that there were people from Eton, Harrow, Benenden, Westminster, Marlborough, Sherborne School for Girls at Oxford too. And I discovered that their schools had not been like my school, but had been ferocious establishments with stone toilets and cod Latin slang for homework and sodomy and common little people like me.

Moreover, the teenagers they produced, although superficially like me, were at the same time bigger, louder, more grown up. They wore tweeds and ties and headscarves: the sort of clothes I'd only seen in period TV dramas.

Westminster boys, in particular, used to send me dizzy with apprehension and self-consciousness. They'd been at a school in London, like me. They'd been just four miles down the road. Their haggard parents hadn't paid *that* much more a term than mine. And yet Westminster turned out a race of gangling, intimidating, hyper-cultured, real tennis-playing giants with basso voices – voices that sounded the way a good piece of furniture would sound if it could speak. What were they *getting* for that extra £200 a term?

Harrovians, on the other hand, were so ineffable, I found them not so much intimidating as, frankly, unbelievable. Six miles in the other direction from my school, Harrow was like a nursery version of White's Club. There was a Harrovian in my otherwise middle-class, grammar-schoolish college. He was very charming and used to hail me with the words, 'Hello, dear boy.' He went on the most extravagant holidays, never did a stroke of work (after one particularly sybaritic term, he was seen preparing for his end-of-term history exams with a copy of *The Ladybird Book of the Normans*) and drank gin and tonics in an unfathomably relaxed and adult fashion.

He had a fellow Harrovian friend in another college. This second Harrovian, far from being a paragon of suavity, was such a fabulous moral degenerate that he could never visit another person's room without damaging it in some way, sometimes even destroying it completely. I was once in the Harrovian charmer's room – sipping a Martini, I think – when the door was practically smashed off its hinges and the crazed Harrovian burst in, wielding a fire-extinguisher. He looked around for a second, saw me, and yelled to the charmer, '*Shall I spray him?*' I cowered in my seat while the charmer pacified the maniac, saying, 'No, no, don't do that. He's a good chap,' and offering the maniac a drink.

The maniac calmed down, had his drink and talked loudly and brutishly about life. Then he said, 'Thanks for the drink,' stood up, opened the door to leave, picked up his fire-extinguisher and let it off all over the room. He subsequently became a Conservative MP.

Encounters like these deranged my view of the world. It was like discovering people from the north of England (another experience I hadn't encountered up to that point), but more distressing. The only thing that stopped me from falling apart under the strain was that mostly these people were never more than acquaintances. High society of this kind was on the outermost fringes of my life. This was even more true when it came to hardcore smart Oxford cliques, like the Piers Gaveston Club (for grand transvestites), the Bullingdon Club (which had been banned from the city of Oxford when I was there, because of drunken depravity) and the Christ Church Beagles (dogs and alcoholism). There was even a club called the Assassins, whose members used to get their names in the papers from time to time when they went berserk and razed restaurants.

These animalistic, high-tone associations were, so far as I was concerned, no more than a rumour, a society somewhere on the horizon. Their activities were distant events where awful people got together to perform frightful acts upon one another. The nearest I ever got to them would be when I came across young, upper-crust men and women wearing evening dress, or some other cabalistic uniform, hurrying down the streets of the town like laughing phantoms on their way to one of their extraordinary rituals.

It was a deforming experience. Not just because it dawned on me that I was nothing more than a suburban stumblebum, but because it also made me realise that my new class-consciousness wasn't a fixed state of enlightenment; rather, it was more a constant wrestling with contradictory moods and beliefs. For instance, having decided by that time that the idea of a social hierarchy based on royalty, smart boarding schools and parental lineage was not only insulting but unhealthy, I started to dream of myself as one of that handful of recusants who, standing in a line of VIPs waiting to be presented to a member of the royal family at some formal occasion, don't bow when shaking hands with the royal personage. Robbie Coltrane, to his eternal credit, once did something like this to Princess Anne. Man is born free and everywhere he is in chains, I thought tritely and high-mindedly to myself whenever I glimpsed a royal movie premiere on the TV.

And yet – at the same time – I too had become majestically pretentious after a year at Oxford. When my parents dished up the Sunday lunch, I would say, 'Where is the silverware? Can we not dine by candlelight, in a more gracious manner? What kind of wine do you call *this*?' I learned to say *yah* instead of *yeah* at Oxford. Everyone said *yah*, even the most keenly meritocratic comprehensive-school boys. We said it because the smart set at Christ Church and Magdalen said it, and it somehow drained like swamp water into the common wordstore of Oxford undergraduate speech. When I met up with a group of former schoolfriends, instead of reverting to the Tottenham-twang nasal weariness I'd had when I left school, I lolled in my chair, holding my cigarette like Kenneth Tynan, The Isis Idol, pouting and drawling and telling them that *yah*, there were masses of girls at Oxford, I mean, really *sexy* ones, and honestly, the whole place was just such *fun*!

What was I? I was a suburban middle-class boy with a gilding of reach-me-down affectations. Anyone at all naïve or socially ingenuous, meeting me for the first time, might have come to the conclusion that I was smart. But I wasn't. I was more like Mr Salteena from *The Young Visiters*: 'I am parshial to ladies if they are nice I suppose it is my nature. I am not quite a gentleman but you would hardly notice it but it cant be helped anyhow.'

Indeed, I had a neat class epiphany shortly after leaving college. I was walking down a road in Battersea one night. A Sloane boy brought me up short and said in the standard Sloane accent, clipped and drawling at the same time, 'Do you know the way to Warriner Gardens?' I replied with my usual repertoire of shrugs and grimaces and nice-guy-but-useless gestures and said no, I didn't. He took a step back and shouted at me, 'THEN FUCKING WELL LEARN!' And sauntered off into the darkness. I was so affronted, so startled, I just stood there for about a minute with my mouth open. There he was, posh, young, fuck-you. There I was, middle-class, young, socially inferior. British society in the blink of an eye.

That's the personal side, the minimally representative first-person encounter with the class system. There is, however, the bigger picture (for which my run-in with a fatmouth Sloane in Battersea is just a metonymical sketch), which involves more or less all aspects of life in this country.

Now, any nation with a lot of social history will have a tidy nexus of power, class and money somewhere at its head. The Germans still have their expensive *Grafs*, the French are littered with *comtes*, many of them doing very well out of wine-making and the CAP; the Italians, typically perverse, inventive, complex etc, manage to support an aristocracy which is both aristocratic and left-wing. And in places with less of a past, the merely rich will naturally establish a social elite of some kind. Even in the States, where there ought to be the most transparent and straightforward relationship between cash and status, money has a way of disguising itself behind East Coast snobbery or Southern plantation-owners' fossilised social beliefs. But only in Britain is the relationship between class, wealth and background so institutionalised, so ossified, so unfair.

Put it this way: if you had to design a society for the twenty-first century, would you, a rational person, see to it that this new model society had all those formal and informal provisions for keeping a tiny elite visible at the top, that our country presently enjoys? Would anyone *design in* the House of Lords? Or a handful of incredibly exclusive private schools to help perpetuate the superior caste? Or a set of social obligations requiring you to defer to ennobled fellow citizens – say, for the sake of argument, the Marquess of Bristol – and address them in speech as 'My Lord Marquess'? Or a monarch who lived in conditions of unparalleled luxury in return for a deeply ambiguous and ill-defined job involving a smattering of public appearances, a few semi-presidential duties and quite a lot of handing out of awards to other, lesser members of the elite? And would anyone sane then make sure that this elite set the tone for the rest of society in such a way that the rest of society was permanently affected by the elite's goings-on, without ever being able to *do* anything about the elite in question?

What's more, would you then institutionalise wealth and wealth-creation among these uppermost people?

Let us take a short trawl through *The Sunday Times'* list of the 500 richest people in Britain. You will not be surprised to find a terrible number of peers of the realm listed there, their extreme richness usually denoted by the word 'landowner'. Certainly, the Duke of Westminster, Duke of Devonshire, Duke of Northumberland, Marquess of Northampton, Duke of Sutherland, Marquess of Salisbury and so on are not cash-rich in the way that, say, Phil Collins or David Sullivan might be said to be cash-rich. The peers' money is substantially held in trust for future generations (unless, that is, you're the Marquess of Bristol or Jamie Blandford, in which case it vanishes like hollow laughter). It's not especially liquid wealth, and anyway, most of it came through dynastic marriages in the nineteenth century. The current owner of the wealth is therefore as likely to be a wastrel or an economic incompetent as anything else, and to lose the lot as a consequence. Wealth is hard to come by and easy to lose. Even the Queen, despite appearing to be fabulously rich – to the tune of £7 million a year from the Civil List, plus money from her own investments, plus the private enjoyment of palaces, castles and retinues of servants – is only really extremely wealthy. She can't actually realise a great deal of money on the staggering assets which are hers to enjoy but not to sell (quite apart from which, she now has to provide vast divorce settlements for her indigent ex-daughters-in-law). It's not a dynamic position to be in.

And yet the fact remains that about one name in ten (by my thumbnail calculations) in the Rich List belongs to a titled person. And by this I mean the hereditary titles, rather than those presents given out to right-thinking businessmen who made a fortune and funded the Conservative Party. Given that there are around 750 hereditary peers in the House of Lords, the overall national distribution of hereditary titles must work out at about one per 80,000 head of population. But among the top 500 richest people in Britain (according to *The Sunday Times*), it's in the region of one in ten. Clearly, some set of rules or values is in place which allows the very grand, by and large, to carry on being the very rich. How ideal *is* this state of affairs?

Of course, governments have interfered with this arrangement in the past. Things have been changing ever since the First World War. Ramsay MacDonald's first Labour government of 1924, and Attlee's two decades later followed by the tax and inheritance regimes of the sixties and seventies, all did something to make society a little more equitable. Even the undiscriminating liberalisations of the 1980s, while allowing the socially smart to claw back some of the money they'd lost in the preceding generations, nevertheless let a mob of *parvenus* claim some elitist privileges for themselves. And then you have such-free market (but redistributive) fuck-ups as the Lloyd's of London scandal, followed by the kind of individual cash crises which forced the Marquess of Londonderry to sell his estate to the man who owns Newcastle United and the Lovat family to dispose, tragically, of their ancestral home. And then you have the Queen herself paying income tax, in her furtive way – not exactly the beginning of the Republican landslide, but a sign of the times, at least. The upshot of all this, according to Abercrombie and Ward's *Contemporary British Society*, is that while in the 1920s the top 1 per cent of the population held three fifths of the nation's wealth, by 1979, this holding had fallen to one fifth.

And yet throughout the same period, the proportion owned by the next richest 4 per cent of the population stayed at about one fifth of the national total. Indeed, the gradual redistribution of the nation's wealth from top to bottom actually halted in the 1980s, under Thatcher, and since then, things have remained more or less stable.

Naturally, the Abercrombie and Ward pattern of wealth distribution is worked out on the basis of numbers only, rather than class. But if you return to *The Sunday Times* you will still see that the richer you go, the higher the concentration of very posh people you find. And for every fudge-brained Hooray reduced to kipping in a bungalow as a result of his Lloyd's excursions, for every denuded aristo, there must be ten, twenty, thirty? toffs doing all right.

Money and class are indivisible. The peers in the rich 500 are without a doubt at the peak of a social and financial graph, but the penumbra of their wealth, like the penumbra of aristocratic smartness itself, spreads down through all the lower levels of the aristocracy, down through society, all the way down to the merely posh. You get it at the top of the pile, where titles and wealth habitually co-exist, and you get it lower down, where the marginally less grand, instead of owning colossal estates and price-less works of art, find nonetheless that schooling, connections, the right voice, all help them to get on in the well-heeled and class-structured worlds of the law or banking or stockbroking or estate agency – or, at the very least, selling flash cars.

So what we have here is not a sensible blueprint for the modern world. It is a rough outline of a large, retrograde, inefficient, structurally skewed society, with a large and permanent element of friction built in. On the one hand, there is an economic cost to all this: one reason (maybe, even, *the* reason) why we keep drifting down the world league tables of productivity, investment and per capita wealth. On the other, there is a psychological issue involved. Posh people, *any* posh people, outrage millions of other people, just by being posh. And it annoys me that I should even be outraged.

Because class – posh and the rest of us, is what it comes down to – is such an issue, both personal and general, people tend to comment on it. At the time of writing, Will Hutton's *The State We're In* was the book of the moment – not because it's about economics, but because it's a book about a society killing itself with its own refusal to modernise. Shortly before Hutton, there was Walter Ellis's *The Oxbridge Conspiracy*, which argued that people like me are at the centre of the nexus of power and privilege (I was flattered). And some time before Ellis, you had P.N. Furbank and his *Unholy Pleasure* . . .

The trouble with the texts on class I struggled with (apart from the fact that there were too many of them) was that either the writers seemed to be worrying over things which to me were self-evident, or that their conclusions didn't agree with my experience. I began brightly enough with Max Weber and his classes and status groups in *Economy and Society*, moved rather more pessimistically on to E.P. Thompson (*The Making of the English Working Class*), drifted through Michael Argyle and his *The Psychology of Social Class*, doffed my hat to George Orwell, skimmed Sorokin's *Social and Cultural Mobility*, raised an eyebrow at *The Upper Class*, by Peter Lane, tried hard and failed with Furbank, and entirely gave up on Tom Nairn's unintelligible *The Enchanted Glass*.

Dead prose aside, the real problem with these class writings is that class isn't something you can write about disinterestedly. It's like trying to write a book about a fatal illness while you're suffering from it. Anyone who talks abstractions isn't doing the subject justice. An example: 'How great is the "social distance" between members of different classes?' quizzes P.A. Sorokin. Subjects, apparently, can be 'asked to indicate how close a relationship they would accept with each individual', the scale ranging from '1) I would marry this person, to 2) I would be willing to participate in the lynching of this person.'

To me, an English person alive at the end of the twentieth century, this makes no sense at all. Class in Britain is a horrible, vital, living thing. Taxonomies and categories and psychometricians' emotion scales don't come anywhere near the constant grinding to-and-fro that British class activity actually entails. Day-to-day class encounters in this country drag along with them a huge aggregate of futile psychological and emotional energy. You can't step back from it and outline it as a set of handily fixed relationships. Your class is your consciousness in this country. Class is *you*. It's not mathematics, or foreign languages: it's what fucks us up.

Orwell, unsurprisingly, was the best, because he doesn't give a flying fart about pretending to be disinterested. He doesn't care about social theory: what he likes is rank polemic. 'The British ruling class,' he writes in *The Lion And the Unicorn*, 'obviously could not admit to themselves that their usefulness was at an end . . . Clearly there was only one escape for them – into stupidity. They could keep society in its existing shape only by being *unable* to grasp that any improvement was possible.'

He goes on to argue – terrifically – that 'what is to be expected of them is not treachery, or physical cowardice, but stupidity, unconscious sabotage, an infallible instinct for doing the wrong thing . . . Only when their money and power are gone will the younger among them begin to grasp what century they are living in.' Now that really moves the argument on.

Actually, Furbank did come out with something I would subscribe to, in his po-faced way. He claimed that 'to use "class" terminology is always, and in the nature of things, to engage in a social *transaction*. Thus if you assign someone to a "class" you are thereby and *ipso facto* assigning yourself and your listeners to some "class" also.' Class observations aren't neutral: they're essentially biased. What's more, class-consciousness is a process of relativities – to the extent that the class into which we put ourselves tends to shift up and down in relation to that of the people with whom we're attempting some sort of social transaction. Thus, when I left Oxford, I thought I was socially really rather special. I didn't go as far as to carry around a shagged teddy bear (*Brideshead Revisited* was going through one of its periodic rediscoveries), but I worked quite hard at pretending to be a posh young git. This madness persisted, on and off, for several years, until I – fleetingly – went out with a girl whose mother had been mentioned by Nancy Mitford (daughter of Lord Redesdale) in the acknowledgements for her book *The Sun King*. The moment I entered her family home, I felt like someone who'd come to read the gas meter. Introduce me to a cabbie, in other words, and I feel helplessly upper-middle, refined, establishment. Introduce me to someone with a mention in *Debrett's* and one of *those* voices and I feel like a cabbie.

It struck me as more apt to borrow Evelyn Waugh's assessment of English class-awareness and tamper with it. Waugh wrote (in the collection of essays known as *Noblesse Oblige*), 'The basic principle of English social life is that *everyone . . . thinks he is a gentleman*. There is a second principle of almost equal importance: *everyone draws the line of demarcation immediately below his own heels.*'

The way I see it, no one I know thinks he (or she) is a gentleman, but everyone thinks that the line of demarcation is immediately above his (or her) own head. Posh people, in other words, start where I leave off. Anybody socially smarter than me counts as posh. Go a salami slice higher on the social scale and you're in the upper bracket, whereas I am still in the middle bracket. This is a vision of society that I subscribed to when I was a sweating, disorientated nineteen-year-old student and to which, after everything, I still subscribe. To put it another way, I, and anyone like me – we're normal. Put on just a hint of airs and graces and you're not like me. You're posh. The invisible wall comes down. Mad? Very possibly – but I would have thought absolutely widespread, and entirely consistent with Rouquet's observations of 1755. How do you know who's posh? You just *do*: it's every Englishman's birthright.

Then I went on to the diaries of James Lees-Milne and it all fell into place. James Lees-Milne (educated Eton and Oxford) was formerly private secretary to the First Baron Lloyd and subsequently a key figure in the post-war National Trust. Lees-Milne also loved toffs and wrote about them incessantly. All you have to do is read one of his diary entries and you know where you stand.

Thus: the Hon. Michael Astor gets so over-excited at an auction of Victoriana at Sotheby's that he ends up bidding against himself. The eighty-year-old Lady Diana Cooper (the model for Waugh's Mrs Stitch) very nearly destroys herself at the wheel of her car by getting her foot caught under the clutch pedal ('mercifully not the accelerator'). When Lees-Milne joins Lady Bridget Parsons for lunch, Lady Bridget – aged sixty-four at the time – flings her shoes through the door before appearing, dressed in a pair of satin hot pants 'and a shirt so decolleté that her bosom was all but totally visible'. She drags a pair of trousers behind her which she later puts on. Lady Parsons and Lees-Milne then go out to the cinema. Lady P. takes her seat for the film, immediately falls asleep, wakes up after an hour, shouts at Lees-Milnes that it's 'a rotten film' and leaves.

Randolph Churchill appears, manfully described as an 'aristocrat' because he 'did not care a damn for anybody; was possessed of unbounded confidence which amounted to insolence'. Lees-Milne lunches with Violet Trefusis and notices afterwards 'a circle of toast round her chair on the carpet, large pieces, crescent-shaped where her teeth had bitten them'. The gargantuan genitals of Sir Harry d'Avigdor-Goldsmid are fondly recalled ('Johnnie Churchill and I always laughed about this'). The Hon. James Smith comes to stay and is barely house-trained: he accidentally breaks the furniture and floods the bathroom, and his dental plate gives him hell as he hunts for bits of food stuck between it and his teeth: 'He makes the most awful gurks and noises, and he ceaselessly chews his thumb. Rather, he puts his fist inside his mouth and lets saliva course down his chin.' And so it goes on.

What a parade of freaks, monsters and aliens! Only the truly grand could behave like this and get away with it. At any other level of society, they'd have been institutionalised or, in this day and age, bundled out on to the street with a roll of cardboard. After Professor Michael Argyll's colourless ruminations ('It is not known where posh accents come from. They could be a hyper-correct version of received pronunciation'), this was the real thing, the red meat I was after.

But this isn't ancient history – this is our living heritage. The descendants of these people are still enjoying the privileges that allow them to behave like this. We have the best aristo scandal-mongering in the world (one of the few things we do exceptionally well, the stuff of much appalled fascination in the continental and American press) because our toffs are real toffs, not just tolerated but constitutionally entitled to place themselves above everyone else, to misbehave, to fail entirely as human beings – and yet still to expect to enjoy both their inheritances and our deference.

But even Lees-Milne's loonies aren't the real culprits, the real subjects of my fixation. The heavyweights, the massively titled ones, are without a doubt crucial, not least because (like the Queen) they set the tone. But they don't impinge in the way that common-or-garden posh people do. They could almost be some kind of gross national fiction, for all the direct bearing they have on my life.

No, the sort I'm keen on are the sort I meet in the supermarket (more precisely, the sort I overhear in the supermarket, braying on at some pathetic shelf-stacker); the sort I sometimes sit next to on the Tube as they frown over their copies of the FT and smooth the lapels of their lovely blue wool suits; the sort who thunderously monopolise pubs in South-West London; the sort who bounce out of taxis with a cry of 'Bye, darling,' and then tread on my feet – the sort, in other words, who remind me on a daily basis that I am a lesser person than they are and that, taken as a whole, our society is based on a system of priorities which clearly made some kind of sense around the time of the Indian Mutiny, but is now a kind of madness, a desperate conservatism taken to insane lengths. These are the posh people who get everywhere and who epitomise, for me, Britain's place in the B-stream of the world.

*

So I went off after them, to see exactly what it is they do to keep themselves distinct from the rest of us; and to see how they get away with it. It turned into a minor compulsion: somewhere between intellectual inquiry, prurience and sheer, middle-class bitterness.

First problem: what were the kind of gatherings that posh people might go to? And secondly, how could I get in? Patently, this would require some research.

I got hold of a copy of the *Harpers & Queen Book of the Season*, written by Lady Celestria Noel. This was a genially inclusive paperback which also called itself an 'Insider's Guide', frankly contradicting the common notion that the only people who need guides are clueless outsiders. This would map out the public side of my year for me. From blazing Ascot ('Royal Ascot is truly that') to some mud-choked shoot ('One way to go shooting is to own an estate'), the *Book of the Season* would help me build my months around an endless sequence of socially smart pleasures. No bourgeois, anal, deferred gratification for me. I was going to leave my suburban fastness and get out among the top set.

(What is the 'season', by the way, in this day and age? According to my Insider's Guide, 'The shape of the social season follows the royal family's movements.' In reality, the season is anything that posh people might want to do. It's self-defining: Ascot, Henley, Queen Charlotte's Ball, polo at Cowdray Park, the Glorious Twelfth, jigging about in ballrooms, killing things . . . Lady Noel even includes The British Grand Prix at Silverstone and the Farnborough Air Show, although it's hard to imagine anyone from the deb class seriously peering up the back of a Eurofighter 2000. Celestria's little joke, perhaps.)

By the time I'd managed to lay my hands on my guide, I found that I'd already missed the Mirabelle Luncheon (hosted by the undead herself, Baroness Thatcher), the House of Lords versus

House of Commons Speedo Swim and the Brittany Ferries Windsor Horse Trials. But this still left me with plenty to see: plenty of other – better – stuff involving horses, water, antiques, the occasional ball. So I sketched out a map of where I wanted to go: starting at Ascot, moving on to the Eton v. Harrow cricket match, Henley Regatta, Cowes Week, the Burghley Horse Trials, Queen Charlotte's Ball in September, a skirmish with Scottish Dancing, Tattersall's Yearling Sales, some charity gift fairs nearer Christmas, and some shooting. This would be my own, suburban season, a *Mon Repos* version of the real thing. It became clear to me (on reading the *Book of the Season*'s small print) that most event organisers want your money rather than your social cachet. If you're prepared to pay enough, essentially, you can get in. The awkwardness arrives when you want to enter the Royal Enclosure, the pass-holders' tent, the members' clubs within the larger scheme of things. I thought I might busk this part and see what happened. I also had a suspicion that if I did get in to one of the smart set's private enclosures, some gang of Hoorays would beat me up for wearing cheap shoes or duck me in an urn fill of vomit, for saying 'pardon' or 'pleased to meet you'. I decided to wait and see.

I similarly decided to wait and see what I could work out on the private side. Clearly, the quintessence of social smartness is as much to do with the private, hidden side of things as it is to do with great ostentatious sprawls like Royal Ascot. So I had to worm my way into dinner parties, drinks parties, weddings . . . how does one get invited to these things? The kind of people I know who throw parties are, naturally enough, people like me. We usually hold events with the emphasis on food and drunken argument, at which we like to kid ourselves we're the bourgeois intelligentsia: cultured, literate folk with opinions on ethics, the global economy, Brahms, messy divorces, lavatories, how much do you really earn; that kind of thing. Fights quite often break out and, one by one, the husbands are led reechily home by their wives.

But smart parties, smart events of any kind, come my way about once a decade. Should I, I wondered, trawl up and down Eaton Square or Walton Street, searching for lighted windows and laid tables and the muted rumble and squeak of class parties and try to force my way in? Should I get a job as a live-in serf in SW1, just so that I could attend, butler-style, at some Belgravia cocktail evening? Should I advertise?

But even then, as someone pointed out, what about *parvenus, arrivistes*, nouveaux riches? If they're not the real thing, how do you tell what is? How do you distinguish between the merely conspicuously well-do-do and authentic Sloanes? What about that radical Thatcherite argument of the 1980s, which propounded the idea of wealth pouring into new and previously untouched corners of society, causing the old priorities to break down?

To be honest, I thought I'd let them tell me. Enough people, I reckoned, would tell me that this was the way it worked for me to triangulate some kind of bearing. What I needed to do was get in among them, breathe their atmosphere, listen to their conversations. Be a spy. And as it chanced, something did work itself out.

T<u>WO</u>

I was at Ascot. Walking through the main entrance to the course, I made my way past a notice which read 'NO £50 NOTES, T-SHIRTS, SHORTS.' A few feet away, a tall man in tails and a black topper, accompanied by a thin, floral woman, was bartering for a race form from another woman, dressed in a kind of overall and sitting in a kiosk.

'I haven't got any fifty-pound notes!' he cried. 'I only wish I had!'

He had precisely the sort of voice and bearing, of course, which spoke of nothing but privilege and fifty-pound notes: patrician baritone, clear but restrained smile on the face, waves of oiled, grey hair swept back to the nape of the neck, a minute, angular quarter-bow from the waist as he leaned forward to patronise the race form-seller. This is to say nothing of his simpering wife, swaying very slightly at his side like an osier in a breeze.

The old liar then went on, fingering a copy of the race form, 'Tell me, how has inflation left things? Is it *very* much more than last year?' He sounded as if he were talking to his stockbroker rather than a grimly amenable form-card saleswoman in overalls. It was an impressive little display.

Having noted his performance, I spent a quarter of an hour wandering around the back of the grandstand and the rear entrance to the Queen's quarters before going down to the track. I found myself standing attentively next to a fellow who, I was convinced, was a duke or a baronet – he had on the sort of tailcoat that looked too old to be hired, and a black top hat which he wore with a degree of frank, baronial confidence. Bearing the form-card man in mind, I cleared my ears and waited for the baronial man to say something equally class-ridden.

After a few minutes of staring hopefully at him, I realised that it was now time for the royal drive along the track before the afternoon's racing, during which their Highnesses were to be greeted by the cries and approbations of the crowd. We were pretty close to the rails – so close that I was actually in a position to get a good look at the Queen. As she went by, she appeared to be nothing more than a great pile of fag ash: colourless hat, grey hair, pallid complexion, white gloves, and yards of pale, featureless dress, bleached almost white in the hot afternoon sun. She was, I later found out, wearing printed cream by Mr Frederick Fox, with pastel apricot and green, but all this was lost in the heat.

Anyway, the Queen, the Queen Mother, Princess Margaret and the Duke of Edinburgh were duly hauled past in their open carriages, and Baronial beside me raised his finger and pointed at them.

'In ten years' time, they'll all be fucking Indians, all fucking Pakistanis in there,' he said. Then he drifted back into silence. A welder? A used car dealer? I wondered about asking him, 'Do you know Warren Street at all?' but thought better of it.

It was the voice. That was the giveaway, the one true test of class; the only difference between him and the man negotiating a form card. They could have been brothers otherwise.

Ascot, you see, was the first item, the first class-laden event, the first item in my season. And although I had this certainty that I would simply *know* when I got near a posh person, just from the way the nape of my neck bristled and my sense of social indignation rose in my gorge, I found it wasn't so straightforward. Hence the shock of the man who had maintained that the royal family were all going to be Pakistanis.

Once I'd got over that, though, I had something specific to focus my attention. The voice became my quarry. An event like Ascot is so apparently homogeneous that you can't tell who's smart or otherwise just by looking. Hunting around for somewhere to do some more research, I went off to hang around the ring, where the jades were being shown off before each race. This was where things started to consolidate. I made two discoveries. Not only were there the authentic vocalised sounds of the well bred, but the sole topic of conversation was establishing how you were and with whom, and where you were going to be in the immediate future – the only topic, it seemed, for smart people to use by way of small talk. One exchange, between two middle-aged patricians in black toppers, went precisely like this:

'Hello!'

'Hello!'

'Hello!'

'How are you?'

'Terribly well! Super to you see you!'

'Where's your lady wife?'

'Arabella?'

'Arabella.'

'*Arabella*. She's over there, she's right up there.'

'Oh, right, she's over there.'

The chap married to Arabella pointed in the direction of the Tote board.

'Yes, she's over there, right now. *I'm* going over there in a minute.'

There was an infinitely small pause. Then the man who wasn't married to Arabella leaped in and repeated the question he'd started off with.

'So how *are* you?'

'Terribly well! How's things?'

'Good, super!'

At this point it must have struck them that if they weren't careful they'd find themselves stuck on a permanent loop, defying the conventions of time and entropy. Arabella's husband broke the chain.

'Well, we keep using this channel, so we'll see you again, I expect, ha, ha!'

'Yes!'

'Goodbye!'

'Goodbye!'

A generation ago, at Ascot people looked the same and undoubtedly were the same. Someone called Sir Tobias Clarke was recently quoted in a glossy mag as saying: 'When I first went to Ascot there were only three people wearing grey morning suits and one man always wore a brown frock coat.' It must have been a sea of black, like a state funeral. Nowadays, about 40 per cent of men in morning suits wear grey at Ascot, the rest black. But even allowing for this marginal variation, a morning suit is still a remarkably standardised piece of clothing, especially when there are thousands of them in one place, being worn by dukes, house-breakers and suburban dentists. I did spot a cleric in some sort of bizarre *Barchester Towers* frockcoat and dog collar, to vary the tone. And I also saw, in the Royal Enclosure, a tough-looking, thickset bloke with a beard and an outfit of mildly distorted Teddy-boy drapes. Otherwise, everyone had been dressed by the same mono-maniacal outfitters (Moss Bros alone hired and fitted 300 morning suits on the Monday before Ascot) and the effect was a cross between Bond Street, 1912, and China at the time of the cultural revolution.

The women, conversely, could be interchangeably wearing anything from microskirts and brutally padded jackets to sweeping floral ensembles made from the bedroom curtains; to inchoate, sack-like things as worn by the Queen herself. Just as they now let divorcees and Joan Collins and women in trouser suits into the Royal Enclosure, there seem to be no specific dress rules for women, other than not to look too much like a relapsed alcoholic. As a result, there was uniformity in diversity. Any female, wherever she came from, could be wearing anything.

I should explain, incidentally, that I was wearing a creased, filthy, linen jacket, a pair of heavily stained off-white trousers, dirty brown shoes and a wool tie. I looked like a municipal gardener going to an extremely rough wedding reception. My thinking behind this was that since I hadn't got a ticket for the Royal Enclosure (the only place at Ascot which obliges you to wear a morning suit), I wouldn't need to dress up. So I thought I'd just arrive with the rest of the mob, absolved of any need to look smart.

But the rest of the mob, whatever kind of pass they had, were wearing tailcoats and fuchsia dresses and unaccustomed hats.

Indeed, I spotted this the moment I boarded the Ascot special train at Waterloo. It was filled with brazen Irish fellows conning the *Racing Post*, peering at the darkening sweatbands of their toppers and saying, 'Jesus Christ, I'll never keep this bloody thing on all day.' There were also many nicely turned-out women, in knots of three and four, peeling their tights away from their damp ankles and trying to fan their bosoms with what free folds of dress they could find. A trio of ladies sitting opposite me started to unpack a picnic lunch as we drew out of Clapham Junction. By the time we pulled into Richmond Station, still miles from Ascot, they were eating Scotch eggs and drinking white wine.

Quite clearly, not all these people were Royal Enclosure pass-holders. They couldn't have been. There were reading the *Racing Post* and talking about their bosses. I thought I'd made a rational decision, wearing my dirty old gardener's outfit. And then I found all these characters from *Keep the Aspidistra Flying*, done up for an imaginary society wedding. I knew that Ascot (like Glynde-bourne) is one of those senselessly dressed-up English occasions (for the Prix de l'Arc de Triomphe, by way of contrast, the French make do with business suits and cocktail frocks), and I knew perfectly well that thousands of men would be wearing morning dress. But I didn't anticipate quite how many thousands. This was why the voice came as such a relief. The whole thing had been in danger, up to that point, of becoming nothing more than a clamorous blank.

Emboldened by my encounter with the two Arabella obsessives, I moved over to the Garden Bar (open only to Royal Enclosure pass-holders, but where, nonetheless there was only a knee-high paling between me and its occupants). Two women were sitting there, locked in conversation. I stood just behind them, greedily

scribbling their exchange in my notebook. The first one said:
'I'm going to join you.'

The second one said: 'Oh good! I hate being on my own.'

'So I'll meet you over there.'

'Over there.'

'I'll meet you over there.'

'Oh, well, that's terribly good!'

'Are you going over there now?'

'Yes, I'm going over there.'

'So I'll meet you there.'

'I'll meet you there, then.'

In both cases – Arabella's friends and the two women – I thought at first that my hearing was going; that maybe I was tuning in only to snatches of the conversation, the unsuspenseful, limply declarative bits. I thought that I must have been missing the argumentative, engaged, revelatory side. But it wasn't my hearing at all. These conversations were complete. The whole point seemed to be to keep the exchange ticking over without committing oneself to anything so rash as an idea. In contrast, mark you, the riff-raff of the Ascot crowd were busy getting drunk and having – no, shouting – dialogues with each other in which they swore and cackled with laughter and took up violently contradictory positions and got tangled up in their initial hypotheses ('Look, if the Queen owns Phantom Gold, she *can't* own Moonax, can she?'). Their faces were far more mobile than those of the posh. Their voices were louder. They laughed like machine-guns.

But the posh people, the smart set, said nothing at all, in a constant, gentle swell of verbiage. The men, in particular, got extra mileage out of it by doing everything fantastically slowly; talking, moving, laughing (*hur, hur, hur,* delivered like a tape-recording at the wrong speed). They walked with what is apparently known as the Guardsman's Gait, a kind of stiff, funereal shuffle, with an imaginary sword held at the waist. It was as if they were wading through a sea of gelatine, reciting their diary engagements for the next five years.

Apart from checking on where they were and where everyone else was, they could also protract reality by describing events to each other in real time, to people who were witnessing the same occurrences right next to them. I lurked, not quite able to believe what I was hearing, behind a morning-suited old boy and (I guess) his old, hatted and flowered wife as they watched the horses being led from the paddock out on to the track.

'There's five,' said the old boy, as horse number 5 went past.

'Yes, there's five,' agreed his old girl.

Number 24 went past.

'There's twenty-four,' she said.

Number 24 frisked around a bit and tried to bite the stablegirl leading it.

'He looks a bit green,' said the old boy, as the horse fizzed away.

'A bit green,' echoed the old girl.

'Yes, he's definitely a bit green,' agreed the old boy, agreeing with the old girl who'd just agreed with him.

'Oh! There's nineteen,' she said, as horse number 19 duly emerged.

And so it went on, until all the horses were out and the temporary barrier which the course officials had put up to part the crowds was taken down. At the start of this process the old girl said, 'Oh! We're not allowed to go.'

By the time she'd finished her sentence, the barrier had been removed. The old boy at once seized on this change, and observed, 'Now we can go.'

The old girl nodded her head. 'Now we can go.'

What can it be like, living in this endless, verbalised, continuous present? Of course, an event like Ascot is not real life, and quite normal people behave oddly in such situations. Even the couple commentating on horse numbers couldn't have spent their entire lives saying, 'I'm opening the car door.'

'Oh yes, look, the car door's opening.'

Or, 'I'm about to have a thought.'

'Are you about to have a thought?'

'Yes, I'm about to think that I'm going to put that slice of fish in my mouth.'

'Oh, yes, that slice of fish there . . .'

Clearly, at a social gathering like Ascot which rambles on for hours, with no really diverting central theme or argument, you try to keep the conversation going without letting it get fixated on a point. But middle-class people like me feel a constant need to attempt to say something meaningful all the time. I never achieve it, of course, and end up mouthing boring pretensions, but I can't stop feeling that I ought to try. Until Ascot, however, I'd never heard anyone so scrupulously avoid the implications of passing reality that their conversation ended up like a series of exchanges in a Teach Yourself Italian course.

The funny thing is, it works. Provided, that is, that you're not doing anything complicated, and that all parties give up their intellectual self-consciousness and simply persist in articulating the present.

I tried it experimentally with my wife later on, and it passed the time quite nicely: it gave me plenty of mental space to have thoughts about things other than those which were happening directly in front of me, but kept up the sensation of pleasurable social intercourse. Time drifted past in a sort of mantric haze. I even started drawling a little and stooping from the waist, just to heighten the effect. In fact, it was all going marvellously until I found that I wasn't exercising the kind of subliminal self-censorship that smart people obviously use as a control on their commentaries. It was when I began saying things like, 'I think I'll go to the lavatory, now. Yes, my bladder's fairly full. I definitely think I need to go for a pee,' that it all fell apart and my wife had to cuff me round the back of the neck to bring me back to normal.

These Ascot conversations fulfilled two essential functions: they acted as class markers, differentiating the socially smart from the merely well turned-out, and they kept things going pleasantly. Given these peculiarly narrow requirements, they couldn't have been quite normal, even for posh people. Nevertheless, they still bore all the conventions of smart talk: the sort of trademarks that, as Nancy Mitford observed, allow one 'U-speaker [to] recognise another U-speaker almost as soon as he opens his mouth'.

I'm talking about elementary things like incomplete sentences ('Super! Super! Must press on! Got to lose some money!'); weird vocables ('hice' for house, 'strawdinreh' for extraordinary, 'Quinmahthah' for Queen Mother); emphases signalled with piledriver deliberation ('That is SUCH fun! Are you REALLY going to do it? You're SO lucky! Isn't she looking MARVELLOUS?'); the clear, well-articulated confidence that what you say is worth saying, no matter how ludicrous it may have sounded to a sceptical little tick like me; and a general sense of being *up*, of being a good sort and not picking at things in a nasty, pimply sort of way, or blurting out importunate questions about other people's health, marriages, herpes, alcoholism, etc.

From this point on, the voice became my touchstone. The voice is incontestible: the one class identifier which can't be traded, sold or borrowed. The voice is the difference between officers and ranks, between waiters and waited upon, between judge and accused, between superior and inferior. It's the difference between Labour and Tory backbenchers in the House of

Commons (in itself, about the most bizarrely class-haunted name you could give your legislature). Mad Labour backbenchers make an indiscriminate roaring sound, like stage extras, when they want to humble the Tories. But the Tories have this edge, this braying quality, this snotty, officer-class timbre to their guttural cries across the floor of the house, which always gives them that extra note of intimidation. The voice was what I hungered for in posh restaurants full of suits, straining for the sound of some limescaled dowager complaining that her monkfish wasn't properly filleted. When I lurked around Harvey Nichols in a depressed and seamy manner, or spent an afternoon boring myself at the Tattersall's Horse Sales in Newmarket, if the voice was there I felt myself usefully employed. The voice was a voice I could imitate but never get right.

It was why, when I went to Cowes a few weeks later for the yachting regatta, there was no sense of being in society. Yes, granted, the Royal Yacht was tied up in the Solent, and there is a pompous little Victorian building overlooking the water called the Royal Yacht Squadron. Indeed, as I shuffled past it, I could glimpse a knot of farts, wearing blue blazers and drenched in sweat, standing on the lawn. And I could hear the monotonous drone of their voices – the voice – drifting over the grass. And later in the week, there would be something called the Bembridge Ball, where all sorts of big shots, shavers and porky young girls (if 'Jennifer's Diary' was to be believed) would turn up to parade around in dinner jackets and off-the-shoulder frocks. There was society of a sort.

But none of this escaped into the general environment. Cowes is just a holiday resort, and Cowes Week is best characterised as a week of Fosters lager served in plastic cups the size and shape of a wastepaper bin. Admittedly, there is an impressively titled hairdresser's in the High Street (Paul of Switzerland, Coiffeur Pour Dames) and, when I was there, an elderly woman dressed as

Lord Nelson standing outside a portable office. There were plenty of sailing types shouldering their way importantly through the mob, too: men with walnut tans and NASA-approved sunglasses on their noses and young women in sawn-off denims with don't-fuck-with-me expressions on their faces. And every now and then a group of people in naval dress would fire a small but painfully loud cannon in the direction of the boats (bobbing around in conditions of intense heat and flat calm), after which nothing would happen. But the tone was mainly set by ice-cream stalls and chippies and people wandering around with their navels showing; by the ubiquitous promotional banners advertising Volvo cars and Nicorette give-up-smoking treatments. And it was set by some gleeful yobs who passed half an hour repeatedly throwing someone's bicycle into the sea.

The only thing which could have transformed Cowes from a grimy muck-in to a socially swank event would have been the right noise – the unmistakable noise of posh people together. The only time it came close to this – apart from hard by the Royal Yacht Squadron – was on the hydrofoil across to Cowes from Southampton. I found myself briefly stationed behind a group of Sloanes: boy plus sister/girlfriend, mother and father. They were all done up in complicated dresses and blazers and were dripping with sweat before they'd even set foot on the island. In a moment of touching familial thoughtfulness, Mother gave her son her half-smoked B&H to finish off before they climbed aboard the boat, where smoking was forbidden.

Puffing away furiously before the half-hour trip, Son quizzed Father, 'You know Toby?'

'Yah.'

'Got a great letter from Toby.'

'Yah?'

'Yah.'

And that was it. Toby, the letter, the subject, were all dropped, along with the cigarette butt, into Southampton Water. It was just one of those dial-ins which smart people need to do with each other in order to remain socially alive. No content, no information, nothing mentally compelling. Just some words and the affirming sound of the voice to keep everyone happy before too much silence elapses. It had its own kind of perfection.

And yet, a few days after Ascot, my natural paranoia began to nag me, hinting that what I thought was upper speech – the voice – might not have been upper speech at all. What if it had been no more than a stylised form of conventional middle-class BBC English, practised by essentially middle-class people? What if the Ascot smart crowd had been actors, staging a reconstruction of the opening of *My Fair Lady*?

So I sought corroboration from a woman called Rebecca. She was listed in *Debrett's*, about halfway through. If this doesn't validate her credentials, I thought, nothing will. We sat in a non-smart restaurant. She was in her thirties, unshowily clad in a printed cotton dress. She was quite frank about where she came from. She started telling me about how she'd been to a party in this '*huge* nineteenth-century house in Birmingham—'

In Birmingham? I'm sorry?

'Well, surrounded by Birmingham and other cities. And everyone there was talking about how the family money came from coal, or whatever, a hundred and fifty years ago. Well, ours came from the *fourteenth century*, selling *villages* to the King.'

She smiled, clearly pleased with herself, and took a contented drag on her cigarette. Then an unhappy memory suddenly interrupted her sense of wellbeing. She went on: 'But someone still had the nerve to say to me, "You're just a social climber!" So I looked at him and said, "Where to?" Ha!'

Another profound drag on her cig, then she was off on the question of schooldays. She'd been to some classy girls' school in the home counties, 'not as correct as somewhere like Cheltenham, but more academic'. Among other things, 'We were terribly cruel to one girl whose father was a market gardener from Essex who'd made a lot of money.' She also learned to scorn the boys from the neighbouring school.

'They would come over from the nearby boys' public school – Bradford, was it? Bradley? [Bradfield, Berks, I later found out] And we thought they were . . . well, *beneath* us. Some Radley boys also came over and they were terribly stuck up.'

So Radley's grand then, is it? I'd always thought so.

'Oh, not at all!' Rebecca cried, giving me pitying look. 'Come off it! It's not Eton or Harrow, is it? Or Winchester.'

So stuck up isn't the same as being grand?

'Of course not! You can be terribly middle class and still be stuck up.'

I was nodding hectically through all this, straining to catch every nuance. As I'd hoped, the accent was four-square. House was *hice*; off was *orf*; correct was *crekt*. The emphases were in full working order: *huge, century, beneath*. Everything was *up* – in the sense that things, generally, were for the best. Setbacks and problems (like being called a social climber, for instance) were dealt with and dispatched and one got on with one's life pretty much the way one wanted to . Admittedly, the vocal pace was a lot faster than at Ascot (she was in a serious hurry to get away from me and my mesmerised stare, no doubt), and the content was plainly from another world: instead of merely passing the time, she had a job to do – she had to explain one or two basic points to me, her social inferior.

But there was no doubting the overall effect and the way it corroborated my original feelings about the voice. There was also no doubting the absolute certainty with which she expressed any opinion. Posh people don't hazard opinions or venture possibilities or indicate by non-verbal means that they're afraid they might be talking crap, the way middle-class people do. Even when they're soliciting someone's opinion, they tend to preface the question with an assertion: 'I think Verbier's so overrun with Germans now, it's no fun any more. Don't you?'

Moreover, even when the posh people I managed to talk to were clearly trying to be nice to me, to help me, they would still end up addressing me either in a tone of friendly condescension, or as a father would talk to his earnest but none-too-bright son. I cornered an Old Etonian a bit later on, and even though he was six years my junior, he made me feel about twelve. He was called Tim. He was a nice guy; he worked in the liberal media rather than in anything really crushing, like merchant banking. He was doing me a favour. But he kept saying things like, 'There are three things you *have* to remember,' and (very seriously), 'There's no question, you do get an *incredible* education at Eton.' I was more or less on my knees in supplication by the end of our chat. Later still, I remember a woman practically ordering me to attend the Tattersall's Bloodstock Sales in Newmarket: '*Everyone* goes,' she barked, jabbing her lighted B&H in my direction. 'I mean, it's *mega.*' I went, of course.

I can be categorical about things only when I'm drunk or in a rage. But then, that's the sign of inhibition, overcome only by extremes of emotion or intoxication. Rebecca, the *Debrett's* woman, just like her peers, was sternly prescriptive about everything on no more than a glass of wine and a packet of Marlboros.

But there was another side to it. Because she was talking to me, a prurient bourgeois hack, she knew she had to moderate her position before she became too much like Vita Sackville-West and started referring to her social inferiors as 'bedint'. She obviously didn't want to come across as a monster.

This meant that, shortly after reprobating the Bradfield boys, Rebecca had to do a quick gear change and remind me that she couldn't 'stand all that stuff about the season and class and so on. I mean, I've never even *been* to Ascot or Henley. I mean, I wouldn't even want to go.' I hid my disappointment at this, as I'd specifically wanted to ask her about the drawling top-hatters. It did occur to me that she might have been lying, feigning ignorance as a class disclaimer. But I had to take her at her word, the way one does, not wanting to be unpleasant. Except then I set her off again by asking the waiter for a cup of coffee.

At least, I thought I asked for a cup of coffee, but to be precise I must have asked for 'a coffee'. Not 'coffee', minus the indefinite article (which would have been OK), but 'a coffee'. Asking for a coffee is like saying 'pardon' instead of 'I beg your pardon', or 'serviette' instead of 'napkin'. It is hopelessly *petit bourgeois* and it marks you down as the kind of man who might wear shoes made out of synthetic materials, or take an interest in the Vauxhall car range. Saying 'a coffee' (or even being thought to have said it: I still reckon I just said 'coffee', but it's not something I want to get ulcerous over, not after all this time) is like saying you live in North Finchley. Which, of course, I used to.

So I said it. And she immediately pulled me up on it – I mean, quicker than George Steiner correcting someone on their misuse of the word 'teleology', that fast – and gave me a good-natured wigging for being common. (Good-natured but with a hint of steel; this was a real transgression, after all.) Then she ordered herself 'a cup of coffee'. I sat there reddening, because up to that point I'd been kidding myself that I was carrying off our encounter in a meeting-of-equals sort of way, when in fact it was obvious that all the time she'd been tolerating my presence as a mere middle-classer. And not a particularly distinguished one at that.

Then, about thirty seconds after my gaffe, Rebecca started to tie herself in knots by recounting how two of her 'terribly stuck-up' friends (with whom she had been eating in a restaurant) were talking about why you shouldn't say 'a coffee'.

'They were arguing about whether you should ask for "some coffee" or "a cup of coffee".'

Really? How interesting.

'And they went on and on – I mean, it was getting terribly boring, until my husband suddenly shouted out, in this crowded restaurant.'

What did he shout out?

'He shouted out, "Well, you wouldn't ask for 'some fuck', would you?"'

Good man, I said. The point was well made.

'I mean, what does it matter? It doesn't matter at all, does it?'

We laughed a bit about this, and agreed that her husband was absolutely right on to see through this fatuous social shibboleth. But the atmosphere had been soured, partly because she'd openly acknowledged my bourgeois status relative to her thoroughly established smartness, and partly because she had then compromised herself by running round in circles in an effort to soothe my feelings.

This behaviour became a feature of a number of subsequent encounters I had with posh individuals – a verbal dance performed for me and me alone, my own little litmus test. There would be a tension in the posh person's conversation, a see-sawing between confirming their own poshness (covertly or explicitly; intentionally or unintentionally), and then repudiating it (presumably for my benefit; it never looked much like straightforward social conscience); and then relapsing and confirming their poshness all over again.

I agree I couldn't have helped matters by having my notebook out on the table or obviously tucked away in a bulging pocket. Or even by just looking as if I were trying to commit some-body's words to memory. But they clearly felt compelled to go through this process. Another *Debrett's* woman (I'm not inventing these people, nor a word they say, incidentally: there are just far more of them about than you imagine when you start looking) in one breath told me engagingly and committedly all about a swank dinner party she'd been to, in the next complained that she was 'trying to get *away* from all that. It's such a *closed* world.'

Rebecca even had an attempt at de-Bourbonising herself by sketching in the radical, classless attributes of her friends and family. This person had had kids out of wedlock; that person had gone off to live on the Isle of Orkney; a third had turned his back on privilege and was being an artist somewhere in the West Country. It all sounded very down-to-earth in its way. But the real test of leaving your class behind (I wanted to say to her at the time, but, intimidated by the coffee incident, couldn't find the words for) would be if you joined Marks & Spencer as a management trainee, or got a job with Norwich Union on the personnel side. Doing something mass-market, in other words, something respectably aspirational, instead of playing at painters in a nice old Somerset house bought out of your trust fund. This flavour-of-Bohemia stuff only makes you seem posher. (This is one reason why I could never quite get the point of Tony Benn: ardent socialist he may be, but if he'd really wanted to leave Vis-count Stansgate behind, he'd have run a newsagent's or found himself a position designing bituminised garages, instead of doing the obvious and becoming daffy officer material in the vanguard of the proletarian army. These patricians only give up the perks of high birth when they die).

The voice, naturally, isn't the only on-the-ground test of social standing. At Ascot, the posh-sounding men not only had mellifluous voices, they also generally had something wrong with their faces (too red, cadaverously thin, covered in blotches, teeth missing, corpse-like pallor) and almost universally had disgusting hair (swept back from the crown of the head to the nape of the neck in a greasy ski run, plus an autumnal sprinkling of dandruff on the collar and shoulders). The posh-sounding women were generally a lot less ghastly to look at, but tended to have visibly paralysed upper lips, numb with permanent, unhappy smiles. Which must have helped with the accent.

And as the months went by, I found that even if the object of your interest didn't open his or her mouth and didn't have filthy hair, a leper's complexion or a frozen upper lip, you could still look at him or her and discover that many of the posh visual trademarks − as listed in the *Sloane Ranger's Handbook*, among others − were in place.

A resumé of signifiers: posh men, Sloanes upwards, do sport little gold pinky rings with devices on them on their left hands; they wear manifestly hand-tailored suits, never quite fashionable, never quite unfashionable, emphasising the traditional British pear shape of the well-bred male. They wear indestructible corduroy trousers in murky yellow, and chunky pullovers with a sort of regular black fleck on a pale fawn background, especially on nights out in Fulham (is it regulation army issue?). They have floppy, unlayered haircuts until they reach a certain age, and then they start brushing the floppy (and by now greying) stuff straight back, allowing it to bed down with the natural grease and dandruff. And they do wear battered, damaged Barbour waterproofs, full of character and rural dirt.

The women, too, will wear monogrammed pinky rings, but on the right hand. They put visually nightmarish silk scarves around their necks, plus ropes of pearls; plus Alice bands on their heads.

They wear fluffy cotton shirt things with high collars or normal collars turned up, plus (in the country, at least) quilted waistcoats, solid skirts or beefy corduroy trousers (like the men's, only bolder – red, green, daffodil yellow and so on), shagged Barbours and navy blue shoes with little bits of gold adornment. It sounds clichéd; it sounds too obvious to be true, but if you wander around the General Trading Company in Sloane Street, or a high-tone butcher's shop in Tetbury, Gloucestershire, you will see these people wearing these clothes. They wear other clothes, too, it goes without saying – London-based posh women are apt to put on designer-label gear, Joseph, DKNY, Nicole Farhi, gear I don't understand at all – but it's both puzzling and rewarding to see how often the mythical Sloane costume crops up.

But these are merely material things. Anyone mad and determined enough could look posh if they really wanted to. There's a certain artless, muddled quality to it which might take some learning – Sloanes, in particular, like to catch you out by matching, say, a really revolting pair of trousers with some shiny black city lace-up shoes, or a Chanel or Gucci handbag with an old sweatshirt covered in dog hairs – but it can be done. Provided you find the right tailors, dress shops, accessories manufacturers and quality-looks-best-when-somewhat-maltreated look, you can fit the part. You could also drive the same kind of car, live in a similar house, affect an interest in blood sports, *Debrett's* and the countryside.

You could do all these things, *but you couldn't open your mouth without giving yourself away.* Which is why Henry Higgins, in *Pygmalion*, is a genius. He is able to defeat this particular reality because he doesn't just dress up Eliza Dolittle in a ballgown and get her to use a knife and fork properly: he teaches her to speak a version of posh English – to use a kind of voice – which is (we're expected to believe) indistinguishable from the real thing.

This is, of course, incredible, which is why it's fit matter for a play. As Shaw says in his preface to *Pygmalion*, 'It is impossible for an Englishman to open his mouth without making some other Englishman despise him.' In England the window to your soul is your accent.

So how *can* anyone acquire that accent, that fluency with which posh people talk posh?

To some extent, the old fifties formation of U and non-U is a red herring, as Evelyn Waugh pointed out to Nancy Mitford ('If . . . your literary disciples wander out into the English world armed with your lexicon, seeking to identify the classes they encounter, they will drop many bricks'). You can learn not to say serviette, notepaper or 'a coffee', but that's only part of the act. It's not like going to Winchester as a new bug and learning your 'Notions' (a private-school vocabulary, dating back four centuries and last codified by Sir Stafford Cripps). As the author of *U And Non-U*, Professor Alan S.C. Ross wrote: 'The question, "Can a non-U speaker become a U-speaker?" is one noticeably of paramount importance for many Englishmen (and for some of their wives). The answer is that an adult can never attain complete success.'

Once you get past a certain age, it's too much to take on board. You have to know, without thinking, when to lapse from correct speech into deliberate misuse; how to sound *up*; how to drawl and sound as if you don't give a flying fuck; how not to put on comic voices (this is something I'm dismally prone to, but posh people only rarely, if ever, put on an accent not their own; not with me about, anyway); how to talk infinitesimally small; how to tell jokes and what kind of jokes to tell; when to get serious with your special chums; when to talk about your last bit of fun and when to plan the next bit of fun; how to avoid abstractions. All these principles have to be locked deep into your cerebral cortex. They must be at the level of purest instinct.

So how *do* you get this voice? Is it in the genes? It can't be that, when you consider how posh people regularly replenish their numbers from outside the gene pool. Is it in the upbringing? Partly – but then how do you account for the Sloanes who sometimes magically emerge from non-Sloane families? Is it education? There you have it. Back to Professor Ross, forty years ago: 'There is one method of effecting change of voice, provided the speaker is young enough. This is to send him first to a preparatory school, then to a good public school. This method is one that has been approved of for more than a century and, at the moment, it is almost completely effective.' It was working then, and by God, it's still working now.

THREE

Why should Eton and Harrow bother to take over the whole of Lord's Cricket Ground for their annual cricket match? Who wants to see a couple of notorious public schools thrash it out at the crease, apart from the boys at those schools, their fee-paying parents and a handful of old retards who used to be at those schools? How many interfering commoners like me can there be? Lord's holds 26,500 people, but on the smoulderingly hot June day when I went, only – what? – 700 spectators, including the schools' own *claques* of boisterous juniors, could be bothered to turn up for the historically charged 160th Eton versus Harrow match. They could have fitted the whole thing on to Kew Green if they'd tried.

Photographs taken of the fixture in the 1930s show that in those days it drew a better crowd. Lord's appears to be completely full, and there's a good larding of gents in toppers and women in dresses like bedroom curtains, in the Ascot style. Then again, the 1930s appear to have consisted of nothing but large, deferential crowds of people, if you go solely by the pictures: the great age of hat-wearing communality. Do they play this match in public as the result of some misguided analogy with the Oxford and Cambridge boat race? Or is it that even now, we still cheerfully tolerate an incontravertibly public expression of the historical difference between *them* – the superior castes – and *us* – the vast remainder of society, somehow marginalised by the tiny percentage at the top? It's a celebration of a world which ought to have ended about sixty years ago: elitist institutions turning plebians' entertainers.

Still, this was the next big event in my season (end of June, shortly after Ascot) so I had to go. I shrewdly brought some food and drink with me, as well as a friend who knew about cricket and who came with even more food and drink in a conspicuous wicker hamper. We wandered around the echoing, empty stands, looking for a good place to sit. The schoolboys were all herded together like rival football supporters in separate sections of stand, above the main bar. Everyone else was scattered listlessly about, waiting for something to happen. Of the previous thirteen games, Eton had won three, Harrow none, and the rest had been drawn. The school authorities had thoughtfully arranged for a large pink mobile sweetie wagon to be parked in the area round the back of the stands. This was so that the younger schoolboys could get in some practice for the drug-taking years to come by loading themselves up with a hit of pre-cocaine sugar when things got boring.

The older boys of both schools at least had the option of being able to squire an assortment of whinnying girls about the place: sisters and friends of sisters, I guessed. Maybe some authentic girlfriends, too. The girls kept themselves cool in the heat by rummaging through their mane-like hair a good deal. They all had the same way of doing it: forming one hand into a claw, then dragging the claw back from the forehead to the nape of the neck, accompanying the movement with an equine toss of the head. Having sifted their hair, they then spent much of the time milling back and forth along the promenade round the back of the seats, having teenage conversations with the boys. Once they tired of that, they would dive off to a small patch of grass ringed by lawnmowers, motorised rollers and seed-sowers, where the grown-up family members had set up their picnics. The oldsters sat on this rectangle of parched lawn, fiddling with elaborate food containers and looking defensively about them.

My pal and I finally got fed up with looking for somewhere decent to sit and climbed over a crash barrier into a prohibited but quietly shaded bit of concrete seating. Two old boys in chalk-striped suits crept in behind us and each lit up a large cigar. They sat there, placidly puffing away like a couple of two-day-old bonfires. I pulled out some (startlingly rank) blue cheese sandwiches, while the pal opened up a bottle of Tesco champagne underneath his jacket, so as not to make us appear too much like the moneyed layabouts we might easily have been mistaken for. The whole episode was starting to acquire a dreamlike quality.

Some more spectators made their way into our illicitly breached patch and before long, the area started to get quite well populated. There were, I would have said, twice as many women as men in the crowd, generally done up in a regulation outfit of buff-coloured ducks and shirty tops, or jacket and skirt arrangements. Everyone was toting fistfuls of jewellery, substantial earrings and capacious high-tone bags.

Three of these women perched behind us. Feeling like a gate-crasher, I tried not to eat my blue cheese sandwich too offensively beneath their noses. One of the women said to her friends, 'Yah, we're moving on the eighteenth. This *huge* place needs a lot of money spent on the roof and windows. *Far* too big for us, really.'

The cronies said, oh, that sounded *great*, whereabouts was it?

'It's near Bisley. So we can keep up with the shooting. I'm running it as a B&B.'

My ears flapped. I lowered my sandwich. The mention of shooting got me going (money wedded to barbarity, of course), but a B&B? Really? Some Eton or Harrow mother running a B&B?

'I'm taking over a business that's already there, so I shall be busy on my breakfasts, ha, ha!'

What was this? A Lloyd's victim? Someone stitched up by a crooked financial adviser? (A tautology: they are, of course, all crooked. She, as a dimwitted Sloane, was perhaps not to know that.) Sheer caprice?

'There are no pictures or furniture, unfortunately,' she went on. 'Well, we've got the furniture. It's the pictures we haven't got.' She lowered her voice a little and, in a slightly more sombre tone, vouchsafed that, 'Actually, we're really up against the wall on this. Totally strapped for cash.'

This made a change from the generalities I'd have normally expected about the weather, the size of the crowd and where everyone was going to be, and with whom, in fifteen minutes' time. I wanted to turn round in my seat and start quizzing her on exactly how she could afford to send her son to Eton or Harrow at £4,000 a term, while at the same time being obliged to run a B&B near Woking. But then the teams wandered out on to the pitch, to a light rattle of applause from the oldsters and guttural yells and cheers from the juniors. Some scamp in the mob let off a thunderflash. The batting started.

School is where poshness begins. I was told categorically, by a woman who organises charity balls, among other things, that with the right approach and enough willpower and money, you can progress from being common and rich to being acceptably Sloane and rich in one generation; two to be certain. Amplifying Professor Ross's point, she claimed that: 'Your millionaire plumbing equipment-manufacturer just has to do the right things. He has to buy a big house in the country and make sure his wife gets involved with the local ladies. They'll like her, because if she's keen to be accepted, it means that they can get her husband to pay for things like balls and fund-raising events. And he has to send his children to one of the major fee-paying schools.' I thought this sounded a little too transparent, a little too mechanistic a way of negotiating the petrified maze of Britain's upper classes, but she said not, 'as long as it's one of the big schools'.

A big fee-paying school essentially means a big fee-paying *boarding* school, preceded by a small, expensive boarding prep school. There are over half a million pupils at various independent schools up and down the country, but of these, only those schools which belong to the HMC – the Headmasters' Conference – are worth considering. And of those 240 HMC schools, only about 25 really deliver the social goods. London, for instance, is full of fee-paying day schools, but the only one which turns out real class ogres is Westminster (Harrow, of course, is boarders only, which helps to explain why its pupils are the way they are).

This is one very good reason, perhaps *the* reason, why I could never cut it as a posh person. However fee-paying my school was, it was unquestionably a suburban boys' day school. It was full of children whose parents were dentists, self-employed accountants, GPs, builders, suburban solicitors (like my father), car dealers. The philosophy of life of this generation and class (*normality through averageness*) was transmitted pretty effectively by the school during daylight hours, then continued at home through the medium of the TV (*Dad's Army, Top of the Pops* and *The Morecambe and Wise Show*), food (packet Swiss rolls, chops, nothing common like chips in an open wrapper), teenage leisure (borrowing Mum's car, cheap, raddled DIY parties in other people's houses, warm Party 7 nursed in a corner, cig butts in the peanuts, driving home drunk) and culture (Rachmaninov's Second Piano Concerto in the long-player collection; Agatha Christie and Georgette Heyer on the bookshelves). No one at my school could have been called remotely socially smart. Several pupils, indeed, were clearly distant relations of Arthur Mullard.

The right way to go about it – a way which would doubtless have worked for me as it has worked for thousands of now-posh children – is to go to a boarding prep school (Summer Fields, Ashdown House, the Dragon School, Ludgrove; any one of the heavy hitters for little boys) at the age of seven or eight, and be vaccinated against *petit-bourgeois* tendencies. Once in this system, your smart prep-school inmates are fed a diet of accelerated ageing (deserted by Mummy, surrounded by vicious small boys, acres of marshy playing fields cutting you off from the modern world – the same conditions faced by a first-timer in jail), formal and informal instruction in how to speak with the voice and senseless but character-building attention to form.

I met a bloke who'd taught for a term at one of these institutions (a Lancing man, actually: bespectacled, donnish, seven feet tall, voice like a church organ) who explained that the first thing the *homunculi* in his charge had to do on arrival at the school was to sort out their tweed jackets. 'They all had to dress like little middle-aged men, and had these bristly little jackets made for them. The jackets were so short and square and the material was so stiff that you didn't need to hang them up. You could just stand them up on the floor in a line and they wouldn't fall over.'

If you survive the shock of being abandoned in a home-counties prison with only a reinforced tweed jacket to comfort you, you will then meet other girls and chaps whose parents are Sloanes or more. This is useful if your father is a scrap dealer, say, and would not normally be in a position to help you mix with the top set. The drawback is that if your background is wealthy but hopelessly *déclassé* (like the market gardener's daughter at Rebecca the *Debrett's* woman's school), or your dad is poor and not socially smart, you will get your head kicked in.

The other drawback is that boarding prep schools – and, yes, boy's boarding prep schools in particular – do seem to attract a certain type in the master's common room. I know this is one of those vicious calumnies which prep school heads and the Incorporated Association of Preparatory Schools have been refuting for years now, but all I can say is that Tim, the Etonian who made me feel twelve years old, went to one of these places. Looking back on his schooldays from the tranquillity of a Sloane-rich pub off Campden Hill, he seemed quite matter-of-fact about it. His line on the whole experience was this:

'I went to a very proper prep school, a feeder for Eton, Winchester, Marlborough. It was full of middle-aged men who liked to be around small boys, basically. One of them would give you a sherbert dab if you let him put his hand down your trousers.'

Like any middle-class liberal, I made all sorts of gestures of horror, disgust, amazement, etc. at this, before indicating to Tim the Etonian that I wasn't averse to hearing more. So it was what, packed with Captain Grimeses, then?

'Another one used to sit on the edge of the bath and say, "Have you washed your privates? Show me."'

Actually, I can remember someone like that at my school, when I was nine or ten. He was reputed to have a steel plate in his head, but whether or not he did, he certainly hung around the school baths after football and diligently fished the soap out of the flocculent, boy-infested waters. Not quite in the league of the original model for Captain Grimes (revealed in Waugh's *A Little Learning*: 'I took Knox Minor away behind some rocks. I removed his boot and stocking, opened my trousers, put his dear little foot there and experienced a most satisfying emission'), but enough for me.

As if that wasn't bad enough, Tim the Etonian then had to have his personality rearranged by 'a tremendous amount of beating. I was beaten on my first day there. The master said, draw a lattice. I thought he said lettuce, so I drew a lettuce. He thought I was taking the piss, so he bent me over his knee and beat me with a metal ruler. Another master had a cupboardful of canes of different sizes . . .'

I looked at him speculatively. It was turning into a typically skewed conversation. He *looked* perfectly normal – low-key media chino trousers, chainstore polo shirt, directionless hair – a bit like me, in fact. But that class training, that Etonian core, meant that whenever he opened his mouth, it was quite clear that any kind of self-doubt, any confusion about his purpose in the world, just didn't get a look-in. He even sat on his pub bench with a kind of extra solidity. He gave the impression of having been internally constructed by craftsmen, rather than allowed to assemble himself, amateurishly, as I had.

I should also point out that all his prep-school depravities took place some twenty years ago. Since then, corporal punishment has been dropped (the public schools falling into line with the general provisions of the Education Act 1986, which abolished corporal punishment in state schools), standards have changed, institutions have become less diabolical (prisons, hospitals and the police force excepted, of course). No doubt the pederasts and sadists are long gone. And the days when 'Whacker' Chenevix-

Trench ruled at Eton are now no more than the stuff of heated debate between Paul Foot (who was beaten by him at Shrewsbury) and other victims of Chenevix-Trench's flagellation obsessions. But their products, their former responsibilities, are alive and gearing up to rule the country – psyches presumably distorted beyond comprehension by what happened to them in childhood. Wasn't Tim, fundamentally, mutilated by his experiences?

'Well, the thing is,' he said, drawing contemplatively on a cigarette (do all posh people smoke? The answer is, essentially, *yes*), 'you assume that, because it's the only world you know, the rest of the world is just the same. And believing that means that you don't question, you don't worry.'

And afterwards? Don't you emerge into the real world and experience the hideous re-ordering of hindsight? What did you feel when you discovered that society wasn't made up entirely of people who'd been wrenched from their families at the age of eight, masturbated by middle-aged strangers and hit with steel rulers? Didn't it make you wonder whether the savage journey from boyhood to puberty had really been worth it?

'No,' he said. 'It wasn't a problem at all.'

I sat and waggled my eyebrows in a vaguely sceptical, vaguely incredulous manner, but he was impervious. He just looked coolly, Etonishly, at me.

And then, aged thirteen, you have to go to one of *those* schools, one of those whose very names are a shorthand for a kind of class-consciousness. By now, after five years of concentrated immersion in prep school, the voice should be not merely second nature: that voice is your voice. You can't do anything but talk posh. You won't lose it when you go home, even if your father talks like Jimmy Nail. You have those sounds lodged in the most primitive part of your brain, along with the basic functions of breathing, trying to get hold of some ready cash, voting Conservative.

But you also have to take exams and work your way into a grand boarding school, a place where you may or may not learn much, but are inducted into society. The grander the school, the smarter the society. And here I admit a difficulty. I don't understand the hierarchy of grand boarding schools, the relationships they bear to one another. This is no more than a reflection of the fact that I'm a dyed-in-the-wool outsider, but, for whatever reason, I can't get the league table clear in my head. It confused me when *Debrett's* Rebecca claimed that Radley wasn't socially one of the top schools, and it still confuses me.

Eton is clearly your top school, bearing the same relationship to other posh schools as the royal family does to the rest of Britain's aristos and toffs. Made of the same clay, but transfigured into something other, and transforming those who've been through its mill. But once you get below Eton, I find it increasingly hard to know what's dead posh, what's merely posh, and what's no more than socially tolerable. The main reason for this is that I meet so few public-school heavyweights in my daily, suburban round. As far as I know (some of them may have been concealing their origins, of course) my tally, in post-university life, of grand school acquaintances amounts to two from Eton (three if you include the man who drew a lettuce), one from Marlborough, one from Charterhouse, one from Radley, one from Shrewsbury, one from Sherborne School for Girls, one from Heathfield, one from Benenden (I think), one Lancing, one Harrow and one Westminster. I've never wittingly met anyone who went to Winchester, and have since formed only the most speculative impression of the place: that it's full of young treasury officials who look like Richard Wattis and spend their time doing Latin acrostics.

As for the other schools, I don't really know which are

seriously grand, and which just have good PR. Returning to
Radley: the school was on the TV years ago in a weekly fly-on-
the-wall documentary series. This made the place look so lan-
guidly, unreally posh that it came over as a cross between
Cambridge University and a long holiday in Burgundy. This was
principally where I got the idea that it *was* posh. Shrewsbury, on
the other hand, was completely unknown to me for years – I
mean, I don't think I even knew there was a posh boys' school in
Shrewsbury until I met an ex-Shrewsbury person, or Old Salopian, as they're known (Downhill Salopian, ha, ha, is their joke),
who turned out to be one of the most bumptious, condescend-
ing dickheads you could wish to encounter. 'Do you *have* a car,
Charles?' is the sort of question he would come out with, laden
with implied insult. So I now know that Shrewsbury is a school
to be reckoned with.

The Marlborough guy, conversely, is both grand and charming.
Now, is that no more than his native style, or is it because Marlborough made him that way? Am I impressed by him simply
because I have Marlborough in my head as being *up there* along
with Eton, Winchester, Westminster, one of those irrefutably smart
institutions, and am projecting this on to him?

And what about places which, even when I've heard of them,
give me the feeling that I haven't really heard of them? Places
with no resonance at all. For example, this Bradfield College
('traditional public school which still retains totally male atmosphere' according to the *Good Schools Guide*), or somewhere called
St Edward's, apparently popular with Sloanes whose boys don't
get into Eton or Radley ('traditional belief that Teddy's is more
brawny than brainy is dying,' *GSG*, page 372), to say nothing of
West Heath School for the Daughters of Gentlefolk, where
Princess Diana went, or St Mary's Convent, Ascot, for Catholic
girls ('an oasis of tranquillity')?

Are you supposed to have an opinion on all these places, not just on Eton and Winchester? A woman called Charlotte (*Debrett's* again, number three on the list), who'd been to Sherborne School for Girls, told me that when younger, she used to ask people she encountered for the first time which school they went to. What's more, 'At university, I used to meet people who hadn't been to a public school but were clearly cleverer than *me*! I couldn't *believe* it!' Sherborne, incidentally, is known as *the potting shed of the English rose*. Charlotte fondly recalls spending Sunday evenings sitting in the headmistress's study, practising the art of conversation. 'You were allowed to do sewing at the same time, but not knitting.' Ludicrous? Or is it just me?

(On the subject of girls' schools, I might as well say, parenthetically, that this conspectus features almost no girls' schools. Why not? Because the posh women I encountered seemed to have a much more tenuous link with their schools than their male equivalents; because posh girls, until recently, haven't been *expected* to do much at school; and because clever, ambitious posh girls often end up at boys' schools. Rugby had a head girl at the time of writing.)

Do you have to have every school of any importance categorised by rank in your mind? Is that part of the social cultural package? Do they teach you precisely where your smart school is in relation to all the other smart schools? Does some master stand in front of the board with a lecturer's stick in his hand, rapping out mnemonics (BUSH: Beneath Uppingham Stands Haileybury; ALES: Ampleforth's Left-Footers Equal Stonyhurst's; SOD HARROW: Stowe, Oundle and Downside Have Always Ridden Roughshod Over Wellington), while the Lower Fifth painstakingly copies it out in longhand?

Eton's top. It has these enormous ancient buildings and vast reserves of cash, and Prince William goes there. But even if he didn't, the sheer weight of horrified fascination that Eton attracts would make it a cynosure. What's more, anyone who's had any contact with the place seems compelled to write and talk about it, at length, afterwards. Accounts follow the *Divine Comedy* schemata, ranging from the infernal through the merely tortured to the paradisiacal.

Jonathan Gathorne-Hardy, for instance, gives Eton the full depraved madhouse treatment in his epic *The Public School Phenomenon*, dilating on the Long Chamber – a vast, cloacal dormitory where, in the eighteenth and nineteenth centuries, some fifty scholars used to sleep.

'For over a century,' says Gathorne-Hardy with – basically - relish, 'the horrors (and to some, fierce joys) of Long Chamber echoed in English history . . . It was filthy, stinking of corrupting rats' corpses, ordure and urine . . . The larger boys, inflamed by drink, could become demons. Bedsteads were crowded round the fires and lower boys (no more than nine or ten sometimes) would be beaten, scorching, from side to side by the upper boys.' This vision of Hades goes on for a while longer, before ending in a resonant, awful declamation: 'They were locked in at eight and left alone till morning, their shrieks of pain and terror, their moans of pleasure, went alike unheard.'

By the second half of this century, the Hieronymus Bosch side of Eton had been toned down. Move on to Danny Danzigger's *Eton Voices*, a Studs Terkel-esque collection of interviews with Old Etonians, and you'll find OE Nicholas Coleridge quoted as saying, with a fetching lack of self-consciousness: 'Craig Brown and I set up something called the Contemporary Arts Society, which was where we incited tremendously trendy people to come down and speak, and hardly a week went by when Elton John wasn't arriving in his gold Rolls–Royce, or Angie Bowie was somewhere around, or Bryan Ferry or whoever.'

Patrick MacNee, on the other hand, slips unbidden into the role of toff repudiating his own class status for the benefit of a lower-class interviewer (Danzigger went to Harrow). 'I'm very Labour in my politics,' says MacNee (like Coleridge, without any apparent signs of irony), 'and I'm not even remotely from the privileged classes – except, I suppose, my great-uncle was an earl, but I mean only just that he happened to be; it's of no interest to me at all.'

It all helps – all this Eton-fixated verbiage, both critical and approving – to reinforce the idea that going to Eton not only gives you access to all sorts of privileges (clever teachers, Elysian playing fields, bottomless social advantage), but actually lifts you out of the mainstream of human existence, redefining you, deeply and ineradicably. Do Etonians deny this? No. They cheerfully admit it. Tim, my tame OE, went seamlessly from prep school to Eton and bedded in nicely. I quizzed him about what he thought about having to wear the kind of junior QC's outfit that Etonians have to dress up in. At first he seemed a bit awkward about shaping his emotions into words.

'I remember walking down Windsor High Street, thinking, not "I'm superior to all these people," but "How *different* I am. Odd."'

He thought for a bit, and then added, 'Actually, I did feel superior. One does.' He gave me one of his more potent man-to-boy looks. 'But you would, too, you see. It's a marvellous place to go.'

Of course. But why?

'The teaching, the buildings, everything reminding you that you are special.'

And the other people, of course.

'There was a tremendous class structure in there. You had to know who was smarter than who.'

You would have thought that at Eton, everybody would have

been too old and too well-seasoned by their prep schools to bother with such things. But no. One of the pre-conditions of being posh involves establishing your credentials vis-à-vis other posh pupils, much as you have to establish your school's exact place in the hierarchy of posh schools, and as Rebecca had to establish her precedence over the other people at her Warwickshire house party. (Your credentials don't need to be established vis-à-vis the rest of us, needless to say, because we're already socially down there with the nematodes and dustmites.)

'You'd make a joke of it,' my Etonian went on. 'You'd say, "My father's a baker" – i.e., he owns McDougalls. Or, "He's a farmer" – he's got twenty thousand acres in Lincolnshire.'

It sounded both fatuous and tortuous to me, but then any society which calls its scholars *tugs*, its lavatories *rears* and its most gilded youth *pop* cannot share the same priorities as the rest of us.

And what Eton does, the other places will tend to do too: in their own ways, they will echo the precedent that Eton sets. You get your grounding – your voice – at prep school, and then you have the rest of your sensibilities radically altered at your great, boarding, public school. And one of the things which determines the greatness of your school is how much and how permanently it changes the way you see everything else subsequently. Do the products of, say, the Oratory School, near Reading ('smallish, worthy', according to the *GSG*), carry the same mental fixtures and fittings of their schooldays as those of Harrow ('very strong, very traditional, very male, *muy macho*')? Cyril Connolly (Old Etonian) argues with suitable subversiveness in *Enemies of Promise* that 'the experiences undergone by boys at the great public schools, their glories and disappointments, are so intense as to dominate their lives and to arrest their development. From there it results that the greater part of the ruling class remains adolescent, school-minded, self-conscious, cowardly, sentimental, and in the last analysis homosexual.' The question is, what constitutes 'great'? Is your school great, if it turns you – convincingly – into one of Connolly's eternal stunted adolescents?

I can remember relatively little about my time at school, except that it was OK, had its moments, English lessons could be absorbing. The best bits were outside school altogether (suburban epiphanies on the London Underground, getting girls at parties, passing my driving test, successfully cultivating sideburns, discovering cheap joss sticks off the Tottenham Court Road ...). On the other hand, the extremely tall Lancing man, although quick to point out that Lancing was several decades ago and hadn't been responsible for everything about the adult man – 'I mean, Lancing didn't make me tall or give me a deep voice. I had those anyway' – could recall his own variation on the theme of How Posh is Your Dad? with perfect clarity.

'There was this boy whose father was the boss of Haywards' Military Pickles. Our housemaster, who was very much a 1930s aesthete, took against the Haywards' Military Pickles boy. He used to say' – in a leering *basso profundo* – '"And how *are* the pickled onions these days? Are they still *good*?" I don't think the chap understood his sarcasm, to be honest.'

Social cruelty from the grown-ups as well as the boys, eh? But that's what the great schools are for: inscribing indelible impressions – impressions which can come, naturally, in all forms. The Radley guy I know (these days, almost worryingly normal) found his life at school being wearisomely fucked up by the granting, of all things, of special privileges. He was made some sort of school prefect when he reached the sixth form, and was allowed to have his bedroom in a housemaster's house, rather than mucking with the other boys. The idea, apparently, was that a housemaster's house, being more closely approximate to a home, meant an improvement in living standards, emotional wellbeing, cleanliness and so on. It was meant to be congenial. The big drawback for the Radley guy (sixteen at the time, and going through a fairly harrowing adolescence) was that he hated the housemaster whose house he was obliged to share. Worse still was the fact that the housemaster's bedroom was next to the upstairs lavatory. And the upstairs lavatory was appallingly noisy.

'I used to dread the thought,' he confided to me, 'of waking up the master and his ghastly wife when I pulled the chain after having a pee in the middle of the night. So I never used the lavatory.'

Instead, farcically, our man used to piss into his collection of coffee mugs rather than use the loo.

'I'd have to line up the mugs on the window ledge outside during the night. Then, in the morning, I'd sneak them off to the bathroom, empty them, clean them with Ajax and put them back in my room. By four in the afternoon I'd be giving someone a cup of coffee in a mug I'd piddled into the night before.'

Agonies of embarrassment, guilt, humiliation . . . but there was worse. Back to Lancing: 'There was this poor guy whose parents had really made an effort, financially, to get him into Lancing, and he was terribly tormented by it.'

What did he do? Rebel? Get into endless fights?

'To compensate,' said the Lancing bloke, carefully, 'he became kind of the school slut. He was known as the Ever-Open Arsehole. He committed suicide a couple of years after leaving school.'

Compare and contrast with what can happen when you leave Eton with your head equally but differently damaged. 'The year after I left,' the Etonian told me, 'two people who were there at the same time as me killed themselves. They couldn't cope with the difficulties of adjusting to the real world.'

Any school can generate misery in its pupils. Any school can be tormenting. Any school can provoke a suicide. But these are the best in the land. What conclusions would *you* care to draw?

These are terrible personal disasters. But the more socially minded among us would also point out that there is a national disaster in all this. First, the nation's best educational resources are biased towards the less than 10 per cent of the school population who attend fee-paying schools, creating a corresponding shortage of excellence in the state system (with all the attendant implications for the nation's capacity to generate wealth intelligently and consistently); and, secondly, fee-paying schools formally perpetuate the old divisions of society into *us* and *them*, keeping that old, stultifying, inefficient class friction alive.

If you really wanted to do something about Britain's noxious system of class-breeding, doing away with the public schools would be one of the obvious starting points. Indeed, it's quite possible to imagine a new social and educational dispensation, if, say, state schooling enjoyed ten to fifteen years of solid investment and aspiration-building, gradually luring the pauperised fee-payers back into its arms. With a really tyro secretary of state for education, you could mount the single most robust challenge to the class system since universal suffrage.

You would, however, have to introduce some element of selectivity into the process, in order to get the pushy middle classes on your side (without their active support the state school ethos will never be properly universal). But this, in turn, could lead to the sort of situation you find in France, where state schooling is the norm, and private schools are considered somewhat freakish. The son of a grand French family I once encountered (triple-barrelled surname, lengthy history) went through the Paris state system quite straightforwardly until some time in his early teens, when he found himself competing in an open exam for a place at one of Paris's best state schools – much in the Eleven Plus grammar/secondary modern style of a generation ago. He got in, and subsequently became a banker – in most respects, the direct French equivalent of some Charterhouse boy parleying himself into a place at Warburg's. Clearly, there is a covert class system at work here, rather as there was with the Eleven Plus. The children of competitive upper-middle-class families do better in these exams than the children of rough working-class families. Thus the structure is deformed in principle.

And yet, even with this deformity, it strikes me that the French system (or the German, Swedish, or Dutch systems) are better at building a society with common aims, values and expectations – a working society, in other words – than ours is. Even at the high tide of Labour's comprehensive reforms in the 1960s, Parliament never passed an act converting the nation's fee-paying schools into state schools. Why not? Because Labour would have lost a large piece of the middle-class vote it then enjoyed. I could have been obliged to go to a comprehensive, or, at the very least to some form of grammar school. And what would that have done to Harold Wilson's ninety-nine-seat majority? So the choice was left open to my misguidedly conscientious parents, who were given the opportunity to pay a fortune for me to go to St Normal's School for dull boys. They took it, much as middle-class parents still do (legitimately enough, wanting a fairly guaranteeable education for their kids: state schools can be excellent, they can be nightmarish – there's not a lot you can do about it), much as posh parents instinctively put their kids down for Eton, Marlborough, Rugby and so on. There's nothing more radical than the kind of education a nation provides for itself, and there's nothing more radical than reforming it. It's just too hard for anyone in a position of power in this country to contemplate making that change.

Anyway, the Tories have been in power twice as long as anyone else since the Second World War and have never shown any real interest in education as a positive good. It's now pretty extraordinary to read in Jilly Cooper's *Class*, published in 1979, her citing of Dr John Rae, then head of Westminster School: 'Except for the inner cities, Dr Rae feels, the comprehensive schools are likely to improve to a point when the middle classes will opt out of the private system, and when they do, it's likely to be in droves.' Was that the last time anyone talked state schooling *up*?

I should admit at this point that I too was a small part of the process of getting young gentlefolk through their educations. Having left university with a swank but irrelevant English degree, I slumped into teaching A-levels at a succession of crammers in West London. These varied from the virtually professional to the plainly criminal. Some had premises in luscious freeholds, complete with carpeting, adequate electric lighting and desks that stayed upright when you leaned on them. Others were in damp, haunted basements, murky with old cigarette smoke and coffee trails, where understandably cynical youngsters would foregather to try to work out by how much each ludicrous educational encounter was ripping off their parents.

From time to time, I would find myself in one of these educational slums, trying to nudge some precepts into the mind of an Old Etonian who'd blown his As, or more likely, an Old Harrovian or Marlburian who had been thrown out for lighting a Balkan Sobranie cocktail cigarette in full view of the woodwork instructor.

Even then, it struck me that Eton turned out a remarkably finished product. An Etonian who had comprehensively stuffed his exams would still turn out to have most of the things you'd expect from an Etonian who hadn't stuffed his exams. I ended up with one young OE who had failed English A-level, mainly as a result of not doing a stroke of work for two years. By the time he got to me, he was a past master at accounting for the absence of the essay/textbook/critical notes that he was meant to bring to the meeting. And he was so charming about it, too. He'd loll in his seat and pucker his brow and say, 'Listen, Charles, I'm rilly, *rilly* sorry about this. I haven't got the essay for you. What can I say? You know? I mean, it's just . . .' Then he'd lapse into a silent torment, puzzling over the exact shade of moral failure he wanted to convey. Finally he would look manfully into my face and say, 'It's just that I had this party to go to on Saturday, in Dorset, and it just sort of went *on*, you know? And I didn't have the *time*.'

The difference in our ages couldn't have been more than about five years, but, fitting the pattern, he made it seem as if he were the more adult one, the one with a handle on the situation, whereas I was the seventeen-year-old rube from up country who had to have things explained to me.

'Yes, but Richard,' I would say, helplessly trying to impose my authority, 'the essay is *two weeks late*. You have *got* to hand it in.'

'I know, I know.'

Then he'd have a bright idea. 'Listen, when we've finished today, I'm gonna stay right here, in this classroom' – a first-floor cupboard, smelling of fungus spores – 'and do it. *Now*. OK?'

So I'd make the fatal mistake of hesitating to consider this idiotic suggestion and he'd leap suavely into the gap, saying, 'No, no, you're *absolutely* right. It's *got to* be done. The moment we've finished, I'll make a start on it. You're gonna be around for a couple of hours, yah? *Great*.'

A pause to clinch the deal, then, like a housemaster offering a member of the Upper Sixth a longed-for privilege, he'd say, 'Do you smoke? Have one of mine.'

It was all done so effortlessly, in such a relaxed, confident and

engaging fashion, that I could never work out a response, Lulled –
and, yes, flattered – by his most winning vocal inflexions, and by
the way *he* was evidently being nice to *me*, I would end up mud-
dling through, doing my best to get him more or less moving in
more or less the right academic direction, like a deferential RAC
patrolman trying to fix some toff's broken-down Bentley.

Harrovians, on the other hand, were more obviously crass
North London types, more laddish in their approach. I had two in
one class for a while, and the only thing that ever woke them up
from their animal slumbers was the line in *Love's Labour's Lost*
where Don Adriano de Armado, the fantastical Spaniard, says, 'It
will please his Grace, by the world, some time to lean upon my
poor shoulder, and with his royal finger, thus dally with my excrement, with my mustachio.'

They thought this was wonderful. 'Dally with my *excrement*,'
they'd chuckle to themselves. '*Bloody* funny. *Excrement!* Bloody
good.' Whenever anyone came into the classroom (another
teacher, an Iranian searching for the English language O-level
class, a sullen new arrival to the English A-level set), the Harrovians would stop everything and, with a tremendous show of
bustling activity, look up the quotation before reciting it lip-
smackingly to the new face. '*Excrement*, eh? And this is in Shakespeare, too! Really! I mean, *excrement!* Bloody funny!'

They spent the rest of the time simply derailing classes by staring intently at a page of, say, *The Waste Land* for five minutes or
more, before looking up with a haunted expression and saying,
'Charles, which do you think is better – a Golf GTi or a BMW
Three Series?'

I have to say that I didn't help by turning up once or twice
with a vile hangover from the night before ('Charlie, old boy, we
think you've been out on the la-di-dah. Are we right?'), and, on
one occasion, by teaching them Shakespeare's *Henry IV Part I*

using notes I'd made on Anouilh's *Vive Henry IV*.

Nor, for that matter, was the atmosphere of quiet study improved by one of the classroom cupboards once unexpectedly bursting open to reveal a recess crammed with African tribal masks, assegais, fetishes and implements of black magic and ju-ju. We were in Knightsbridge at the time. No one ever dared ask the tutorial college principal (who normally liked to put his young charges at ease by talking about fox-hunting) what the stuff was doing there.

What the Harrovians did have in common with the Etonians were the trademarks of the voice, the confidence and the couldn't-give-a-fuck approach to things which I had been brought up to believe were matters of life and death (A-levels, university entrance, keeping your schoolbooks in order). And the only thing any of them worked at all hard at was their social life.

Whereas I considered I was doing well to get invited to some gloomy graduates' do in South Wimbledon, or to a smoggy piss-up in a wine bar, these young men (and one or two young women) appeared to be enjoying house parties in the country, shooting, sailing, dinner parties in town, mild drugs escapades, quite a lot of drinking and driving, trips to villas owned by family and friends in the Mediterranean — the full, rich, adult panoply — well before their twentieth birthdays. Whatever kind of shambles they'd made of their formal educations, they'd managed to take advantage of the incalculable benefits of going to a major public boarding school, and made (or consolidated) the kinds of friendships which posh life depends upon. Their efforts with Tennyson were beyond abomination, but they knew how and where and with whom to have fun.

Was their fondness for self-gratification just a reaction to the savageries of boarding-school life? Or was it a product of having rich, snobbish, alienated parents? Is this why posh people are generally associated with fierce and excessive pleasures — drinking, shooting, sexual profligacy, drugs – because, however materially unruffled their boarding-school lives were, they still lived them out in an atmosphere of psychological depravation and violence? Is there a nexus of some kind, linking school, smart social connections and inner damage, resulting in a desperate and unslakeable pursuit of fun for the rest of one's life?

And does this make the Eton versus Harrow cricket match, with its mixture of hothouse glory and shame, of society, pleasure and latent humiliation, a metaphor for the whole boarding-school experience?

The match itself, having started off at a gentle canter, was getting more hectic. The Eton boys were shouting 'En-ger-land! En-ger-land!' and chaotically attempting a Mexican wave. A large blonde woman in a pink twinset and a double rope of pearls had stationed herself with a lady friend in front of us. We tried not to waft the incense of our garlic sausage over her.

Some more balls were bowled at an Eton batsman and the pink twinset lady turned round to us and asked, 'How many balls *are* there in an over?'

My pal and I looked at each other stupidly and then back at her. She had an expression of patient, sincere inquiry on her face (which bore a high-priced chocolatey tan, I might add). She didn't appear to be taking the piss out of us. Indeed, it sounded as if she was making conversation in the formal manner, tackling only the simplest, least controversial ideas, but with an air of intense interest. Not a bad start, if that was what she was really doing – she could hardly have asked us where our wives were or what time we were going to be standing on the other side of the cricket ground. Checking up on one of the game's commonplaces was a very fair substitute. So the pal took a breath and told her that there were six balls in an over.

'Oh, *really*?' she said. 'Yes, of *course*. Six.'

She seemed so gratified and relieved to find out that there were, after all, six balls in an over, that my pal was emboldened to continue the conversation. He started to explain how the umpire kept pebbles in his pocket, which he transferred, one at a time with each ball bowled, to another pocket. That was how he kept track of the number of balls bowled in an over.

This naturally provided another opener for the twinset lady. 'And which one *is* the umpire?' she asked.

At this point, it all fell apart. The pal, relaxed somewhat by his supermarket champagne, gestured lazily across the pitch and said, 'You'll recognise the umpire, all right. He's got a white coat on, and he's got a face as brown as a tinker's nut bag.'

The twinset lady looked at him for an appalled second, shuddered and turned quickly back to her friend. A frail 'thank you *so* much' drifted back to us over her shoulder.

It was an odd mixture, this Eton–Harrow game, the product of two ill-sorted generations. On the one hand, there were the high-quality old buffers smoking cigars and, surrounding them, the mothers, talking about B&Bs in Woking and enquiring as to the number of balls in an over, while on the other, there were large numbers of young men, inhabiting some unique, horrible, sweaty hinterland where extreme oafishness and high class co-existed.

It wasn't just the firework going off at the start of the game, nor the pathetic Mexican wave, nor the 'En-ger-land' chanting, nor the slow handclapping shortly afterwards, which made me think this. The clincher was a knot of Harrovians sitting in the front row of seats, a few yards to the right of the lady in the pink twinset. When the Harrow bowler finally dispatched the Eton batsman, the boys in the front row let out a baleful yell of 'Ha-rooo', and bunched their fists in the air at the Etonian as he departed the crease. 'It all comes,' said one of the Harrovians in a stentorian voice, 'to he who waits.' They lit up cigs and passed a can of Carlsberg to and fro. One of them then looked up the name of the next Eton batsman, who by this time was wandering on to the pitch, to more cries of 'En-ger-land' from the Eton stands.

'You *suck*,' said the Harrovian, in the batsman's direction.

I was just wondering whether to move to a quieter part of the stand when the pink lady, after a lot of fussing around on the concrete floor, suddenly stood up and said to us, 'Have you seen my *earring*?'

We sat, our mouths full of cheese and sausage, and shook our heads.

'They're *Italian*, you see, and I can't get them repaired anywhere.' She ducked below the level of the seats to where her friend was grovelling around among the sweet wrappers and fag butts.

'What exactly,' I said thickly, 'are we looking for?'

She grabbed the lobe of her ear and yanked it towards me.

'One of these, you see? The other one fell apart this morning, and I was in such a rush that I stuck it together with Blu-Tack, you see. Completely stupid of me.'

'Araldite,' I said. She paused, gazing at me uncertainly. I may have made it sound as if Araldite was what I was eating. It must have looked that way. 'Araldite is what you want. To stick it together.'

'Only if I can *find* it again,' she replied, with some asperity.

Just then, an Etonian at the wicket reached his century. The mass of Eton boys in the main stand went berserk. They leaped to their feet and applauded riotously, their hands held over their heads. Then they then started chanting 'E-ton, E-ton', like a true football crowd.

It was all getting a bit much. We packed up what was left of our food and shuffled out of the stand. The lady in pink had already departed. My feeling was that she held us responsible in some way for the loss of her earring and was looking for a credulous working-class policeman she could harangue into arresting us. On the way out of the ground, gratifyingly, we passed a group of teenagers having a proper, adult orientation discussion –

'I don't know where everyone is.'

'Well, give me a ring, yah?'

– and then it was out into the taxi fumes and impossibly expensive delicatessens of St John's Wood. One wonders whatever happened to the little git who let off the firework.

FOUR

Anything to do with horses is, if not quite generically smart (look at the mob that turns up for the Cheltenham Gold Cup), at least some kind of guarantee of social quality. As David Cannadine puts it in *Aspects of Aristocracy*, 'The ownership of horses was largely confined to the patrician elite, their dependents and their servants . . . the breeding and racing of horses were quintessentially aristocratic hobbies.' I know there are middle-class children who get on ponies and force their parents to traipse around gymkhanas in the suburbs, but, almost by definition, an adult on or near a horse (unless he's a professional jockey, infantryman to the owner's officer class) is posh. You can see it in that terrible litany of the high-quality horse's world: fox-hunting, Badminton Horse Trials, point-to-points, eventing, Ascot, dressage, polo . . . these are things that no middle-classer would seriously volunteer for unless it was a matter of obligation or money. But horses are magnets to grandees, even if they don't ride the things. The

Queen resides at the top, with her stable of nags, and clustering just beneath are names like Lord Howard de Walden, the Earl of Carnarvon, Lord Vestey . . .

And just to reconsider the Cheltenham Gold Cup: if you go there (or to any other big race meeting) you'll find relatively few from the middle-classes, but instead a huge crowd of working-class people and a much smaller, but characteristically essential, mob of smart folk in brown felt Frank Sinatra hats and pricey overcoats, escorting their – frankly – horse-like women from bar to paddock and back again.

Why should this be? What's so special about horses? Other than that the Queen likes them?

Take Ascot: on the face of it, it's barely worth getting worked up about. Apart from the racecourse and the railway station, Ascot is nothing more than a thin ribbon of retail outlets – an Iceland, a dry cleaner's, an Esso garage – a couple of road junctions, and an unknowable hinterland of Tudorbethan mansions and beech woods. When the races aren't on, the place barely exists in any memorable way. A pub called Ollie's Bar & Diner demotically abuts one of the course entrances, and in the middle of the week, the Heath (the patch of land in the centre of the course), is full of geezers walking their dogs and playing golf among the furze.

Nor are the racecourse buildings worth a special trip, being dully crappy in the way that most English racecourse buildings seem to be. Without the brilliant crowds, half of Ascot racecourse looks like an under-maintained Edwardian home counties railway station, and the other half looks like the sixties headquarters of an insurance company. I'm thinking particularly of the main stand, the Queen Elizabeth II Grandstand, which was rebuilt in 1961, with 280 private boxes, masses of horrible blue cladding on its reverse side and a kind of mod Coventry city centre clocktower (with jockey-on-horseback weathercock, painted in royal racing colours) on the top. Around this huge concrete edifice stand the older, brick and wrought-iron Edwardian railway-station structures, housing the racecourse administrative offices, tote counters, stables and an awful lot of lavatories. There's nothing about it which says royalty or high society, other than, perhaps, its scale — and even that is no greater than the equivalent mish-mash at Cheltenham.

The only giveaways are the Royal Box, overlooking the track; and the Royal Entrance at the rear. The Royal Box looks like a Modern Movement fishtank, with plate windows that slide open in warm weather and some privet growing up in front. The Royal Entrance is, aptly enough, a pointedly anachronistic folly tacked on to the back of the modern part. It's a two-storey addition in Lutyensesque brick and stone, through which the monarch guides the various drunks, divorcees and reprobates who are her friends and relations, passing under the carved stone faces of an Indian maharajah, an Aztec, a Red Indian chief and a baffled-looking Negro. The whole is topped off with a couple of neo-classical funeral urns, then it's back to the steel and plastic cladding of the 1961 stand.

There is no hint of that noble tradition stretching back to 1711, when Queen Anne started racing at Ascot. Or to the time when Queen Victoria got so wound up by a race that she pitched herself forward in the Royal Box and broke a window, forgetting that it had been closed to keep the rain out. On an ordinary weekday, shrouded in drizzle, the place has the sad, corporation atmosphere of a shopping precinct with no shoppers.

And yet, come June, without any extra gilding or bunting, it turns into a cynosure, what one overwhelmed hack called in the FT 'The *fleur de fleur* of the Season'. This great, peeling, concrete sprawl becomes a place which compels middle-aged women with sensible jobs to wear stifling rayon and the men to put on waistcoats and thick black herringbone on some of the hottest days of the year *when they don't even have to.* Just because it's horses, the sport of the aristocracy, and the Queen is going to be, in some tiny sense, among them, sitting in her lacquered black barouche or peering out from the royal fishtank with her binoculars at some bet she's made with the taxpayer's money.

Compare this with Henley. Ploughing doggedly through my season, I was now braced for more stifling formal clothes and blistering sunshine, in the form of the Henley Royal Regatta. This always takes place around the first weekend of July, and if the sun comes out at all, it is a killer. So I geared myself up and made my way down the Thames Valley, expecting another bray-session like Ascot, another mass jostle with the smart set.

But it wasn't like Ascot at all. There was something about the composition of the thing, something lacking, which – it took me a long time to fathom out – was all about the absence of horses.

It started when I was having a drink with this chap.

' "Blazer" ' said the chap, 'actually comes from the brilliant red jackets which the St John's Cambridge rowers wear.' He was a tall, thin banker. Bright red blazer face, nose shaped like a sickle. 'And when they row, they have to row under a different name.'

'I'm sorry? I said.

'Because they killed someone in the nineteenth century. And they've been banned as St John's ever since.'

'What?'

'They killed someone on the river. When they were rowing.'

I was finding it hard to concentrate. The sun was beating off the surface of the River Thames like shards of burning phosphorus. I was full of Pimm's and I was wearing black lace-ups, off-white strides, a dark blue wool blazer and a collar and tie. And a cheap straw hat, which, instead of protecting me from the sun's rays, trapped the heat as it rose from the crown of my head, like a pressure cooker. I felt awful.

The blazer man looked at his watch.

'Just got time to hose down a couple of pints and get back to the girls.'

'Aren't we supposed to be there right now?'

'Allowing for leeway, this is,' he said, an expression of rat-like cunning on his face. He sucked down the dregs of his Pimm's and veered off towards the bar as if he were late for a train.

I leaned against the fence which divided us from the tide of humanity surging past. What time *was* it? It felt like midnight, but it was half past four in the afternoon. Enormous figures – men the size and shape of pears a Titan would have eaten; huge women wrapped up in printed cotton, like furniture in transit – drifted past. A cultured voice from a faraway loudspeaker was saying that the University of Magnitogorsk was pulling thirty-two at the Berkshire Station, while Queen's College, Edmonton were pulling thirty-one, and Queen's College were leading by a sheet.

The blazer man swam back into view. He had two more Pimm's in his hands. My cold salmon lunch leaped inside me for a second.

'Well done,' I said, not wanting to be a wet blanket. 'Another pint.'

When Henley-on-Thames holds the Henley Royal Regatta, it's like a man of average build trying to eat a whole pig. About 12,000 people live in or around Henley, a number which quadruples when the mob – riff-raff and smartarses – descends. In normal conditions, Henley is a smug, handsome little town, with a nice old hotel called the Red Lion, plenty of shops selling complicated pot pourri and exfoliants, a steady murmur of Jags and BMWs rolling through the road junctions and a sweet, decaying stone bridge (1786) over the river. This has Isis carved on one parapet and the drugged-looking face of Father Thames on the other. Henley itself is in Oxfordshire. Cross the river and you find yourself in Berkshire, on a bank where, come the regatta, they throw up a townlet of cream canvas marquees, grass enclosures, temporary grandstands and toilets and call it the Stewards' Enclosure. This is the Henley equivalent of the Royal Enclosure at Ascot. Only the Queen never visits it.

Next door to this stretch is an oddly undemonstrative building, a sort of sub-Voysey, marginally arts-and-crafts suburban villa. This is permanent home to something called the Leander Club. The Leander Club is what oarsmen join when they become rich enough to be able to afford the fees. You can tell what sort of mentality Leander people subscribe to when you learn that the club logo is a pink hippo, and that any men you see wearing pink socks and ties (in a pungent, irascible shade of cerise) are engaged in a beefy home counties jest: We're not poofs at all, ha, ha! We're Leander men! Great strapping ex-rowers who've gone into management consultancy and the Bar and have sired many children by our wives and secretaries! Pink, you see? Joke!

The course stretches from outside Leander, downstream for a mile and a bit (and this is why it's at Henley, rather than Pangbourne, say, or Windsor) in a dead straight line. Its end is marked by a delicate island with an eighteenth-century neo-classical folly perched on it, in the shape of a summerhouse surmounted by a tiny temple. And it is down this course that pairs of boats – rowed by individuals, or crews of two, four or eight – compete for the prizes which are ostensibly at the heart of the regatta.

For most of the summer months, nothing much happens, except that Henley goes about its prosperous business, the pubs do a good trade, and a procession of plastic gin palaces churns up and down the river, captained by drunks in spurious yachting gear. The whole set-up is, in its way, very nice, very Thames Valley, very pleased with itself. Viscount Hambleden (formerly W.H. Smith, the bookseller) used to own a swank Italianate villa on the bend just above Temple Island. It's the kind of place that makes you want to put on a Pringle sweater and have a drinks party on the lawn, just for the hell of it.

And then the regetta lands on it like an immense, shamingly rowdy Tory party fringe convention, bloating out all over the Berkshire bank and clotting the town and all surrounding roads with cars and strangers and unnervingly tall fit young men from America. It's not like Ascot town: Ascot is just a racecourse with shops outside it, and, in any case, gets crowds on days other than Royal Ascot. Ascot can cope.

Henley, on the other hand, is a complacent little community in its own right, which is unlucky enough to have this shambles thrust upon it for one frantic week each year, and which has had to put up with it, one way or another, since 1839. Suddenly, it looks like Cairo: the streets teem. Temple Island ceases to be a dainty adornment and suddenly seems out of place, like a lace hanky on a footballer's head. The only real advantage Henley enjoys over Ascot is that even though it's called the Royal Regatta, the Queen doesn't give a spit for rowing, so you don't get that extra, Ascot density of cretins drawn by the gravitational pull of royalty.

(Where it does resemble Ascot is in its massed car worship. To get to the Henley Regatta, you join a tailback on the M4 which, after an hour or so, resolves itself into a jam covering many square miles around Henley town centre and which the Thames Valley Police sarcastically funnel into numberless official and rogue/free-market car parks along the way. You then, as at Ascot, eat your lunch with your feet wedged under the suspension of a neighbouring vehicle.

I lie: Ascot's car parks are so crowded and the visitors' clothes are so refined, that no one lies down to eat, as they do at Henley. Instead they teeter on the uneven soil in their top hats and high heels, eating complicated medleys of salad leaves. And, incomprehensibly, the eaters at Ascot are penned in behind chain-link fences, barely inches from the main road, like hyenas in an open-plan zoo. I remember staring blatantly and hungrily in at them, along with several other derelicts from the street, when I was there. At least at Henley, the majority of the smart set and their lounging Rollers and Mercs are tucked up in verdant fields some way back from the course.

But both crowds have to eat next to their cars. Would you hold a drinks party in the nearest NCP? That's the form. Even at Lord's, at the Eton–Harrow match, the picnickers congregated around the nearest internal combustion engines they could find – the lawnmowers and motorised rollers and so on. What caste impulse makes them do it? The smell of petrol, the muted quacking and honking . . .)

So I went to Henley and did that. In fact, I did precisely what you do at Henley if you're in the Stewards' Enclosure: I blundered drunkenly from one end of the Enclosure to the other, stopping along the way to refill myself with pints of Pimm's from the canvas bars. I also took an interest in the actual rowing, an interest which was so cursory as to be almost insulting. Then I went and gorged myself on a huge picnic lunch, stumbled back into the mob in Stewards', found an empty deck-chair in the throng of chairs which lines the riverbank for the use of Stewards' inhabitants, sat in it and fell thickly asleep.

How did it compare with Ascot? It was a lot nicer, in many ways. For one thing, I was wearing the right gear. I did wonder whether or not it would have been worth the imposture of sporting one of those proper, Henley blazers that real men, real rowing characters wore – one of those cream-coloured garments piped with the fairground colours of the college you rowed for before the bulk around your shoulders slumped to your paunch. And it might have been nice to wear a wrecked old club cap perched on my head like a tiny contraceptive. But at least I had the regulation minimum – the blue blazer, the off-white ducks, the strangulation tie. And this made me feel altogether less conspicuous, less stupid than I did at Ascot.

(A friend of mine once failed to observe even this much, turning up with his gift of a Stewards' pass, but with an open shirt and no tie. They turned him away at the gate for being tieless. Having come all the way to Henley, he wasn't about to go home again, so he went off to look for a shop selling ties or cravats. But it was Sunday, and the only shop he could find open was a chemist's. There he bought the nearest thing he could find to a cravat, which turned out to be a pair of lemon-coloured ladies' tights. So he knotted them round his neck, re-presented himself at Stewards' and was let in. Then he wandered off to look for the friends he'd arranged to meet there and discovered that they'd got fed up with waiting for him and had gone home.)

Lunch – away from the grandest and most overrun Henley parking places – was warm, vinous, tranquil. I slouched on a patch of scuffed turf, trees ringed around me, hills rising in the distance, everywhere Nature tamed by man's art. Leaning against a hubcap, I forked down cold fish. A long way off, as in a dream, I heard the murmur of voices and the occasional explosive bark of someone finding it jolly damned funny to put on his wife's hat and dangle a *baguette* between his legs ('Now that's what I *call* a Fisherman's Friend').

Any grossly offensive people around? Of course, somewhere, but with a *cordon sanitaire* of cars to keep everyone's defensible spaces separate, no one could intrude on me that badly. I knew I ought to have been seething at the thoughtlessness of it all, the sneering hedonism with which such a tiny number of people could take up such a vast amount of space, devote themselves entirely to self-gratification and deny it to anyone else. But, being tolerated, being drunk, being full of fish, I couldn't find it in me to feel anything more than a mild, complacent, well-fed scorn for the other drunks around me.

But even though I wasn't wracked with queasy class otherness, and I looked tolerable (like an extra in a crowd scene, don't examine me too closely), I was still an impostor, and I knew it. What I lacked was that fat joviality, that bulky manliness that the other middle-aged men in the Stewards' Enclosure and the car parks possessed. By midday, all the real men, the over-thirties, were looking like John Bull: crimson-cheeked, bursting from their clothes, one hand pistoning forward in greeting, the other locked round a pint mug. I can't claim to be svelte these days, but at the same time, I don't have anything like the heftiness, the density that comes from having your muscles turn to clay, as had evidently happened to the real men.

What's more, being just a hack, not having a proper job, I couldn't make the sort of big-cocked job-inspired Henley small talk that everyone else seemed to be making. In the Champagne Bar for instance (about halfway along the canvas village), I caught one tubby, crimson-faced fellow announcing, 'I took the Euro-tunnel to go to our Paris branch opening. *Bloody* good. Trouble was, I couldn't get pissed at the party, 'cause I had to catch the early train back. I was bloody pissed off, I can tell you.'

His mate said, 'Any good, the Eurotunnel?'

'Not bad. Bit full of Froggies.'

'Bloody good for a dirty weekend, though. Bang, there you are, hotel all ready.'

The fat man with the red face leaned a little closer to his friend. 'Loads of tarts, too. Round the Gare du Nord.'

'All men, though.'

'What? The tarts?'

His interlocutor nodded.

'They can't *all* be men,' the ruby-faced man said, defiantly.

'Transsexuals,' said the other one. 'From South America.'

Oh hell, I thought. What does one say? How does one say it? *Tarts?* My life is so conventional in its aspirations that the very thought of taking the Eurostar to Paris to get pissed at an office party and find a *tart* struck me as simply the stuff of fable. Perhaps it was equally fabulous to the chaps. Perhaps it was no more than the kind of mildly tanked bravado that any decent fellow would conjure up at Henley in the sunshine.

Even as I worried at the problem, some other chaps somewhere at the back of the bar fired off the cork from a champagne bottle. It whizzed through the air and was caught by a fellow at the front.

'Ha, ha!' shouted the men at the back. 'Caught in the slips! Catch, sir!'

I felt like a cross between a school junior in his first term and a member of the Watch Committee finding himself inexplicably in the front room of a brothel. Normally, I like to imagine that I take a relaxed and thoroughly metropolitan approach to whatever people want to get up to. No prude, me: if everyone consents to it (sado-masochism, Michael Nyman's film scores, soft drugs), then it has my blessing. The British are too dismally inhibited – why can't we be more mature about the moral ambiguities of life, like the continentals? That kind of thing. But once I found myself surrounded – utterly surrounded – by thousands of Hoorays, all bent on loosening up after a hard week of debt-refinancing, I froze. I became hopelessly priggish.

★

This was not just me lapsing into an adolescent attack of consciousness-of-being. Henley *is* a horribly male event. At Ascot, women are much more central. They wear short skirts. There are thousands and thousands of them, looking, generally, lush. They also have *fun*: betting, drinking, flirting, shouting and laughing. Whether you actually enjoy Ascot is a matter of taste and background. But the atmosphere is much sexier.

Henley is both hearty and dowdy in comparison. The women are repressed and the men are encouraged to treat the whole thing as a mass excursion to the pub. You do get pretty girls in the Stewards' Enclosure, but the rules governing women's dress are depressingly stuffy: skirts must reach over the knee; no split skirts; no trousers. Nineteen-fifties garb preferred. No visible thighs, and, by a process of extended self-censorship, no cleavages. The men, although submitting to a dress code of collars, ties and jackets, can wear the most revoltingly shabby clothes as badges of pride. Shitty rowing blazers – really horrid, shagged old garments, fading, split, the seams in distress – are not, like my jacket at Ascot, something to be ashamed of, but tokens of belonging.

The sport itself is on the earnest, masculine side, too. No betting, no glossy, capering horseflesh (although some of the oarsmen have a pinheaded, beefcake quality to them), no bright silks on the jockeys' backs. Just blokes in invisibly slender boats, sweating and grunting, watched by an audience of bored girls and other blokes, many of whom have also sweated and grunted in their time and are seizing the chance to be free for a day and drink too much and sweat and grunt in remembrance of their youth, as they wrestle their way to the bar. You have to have a special take on the rest of the world to wring much satisfaction from that.

Now, I could see that this stuffiness, this relative shabbiness, actually makes Henley posher than Ascot. The faded heirloom qualities of the men's clothing, the huge but rustic tents, the field-station bars (staffed by well-spoken home counties boys and girls), the dusty turf and the gentility of the ladies' dress – the sense of all social change having been suspended – in many ways make Henley far more authentically smart than Ascot, where the smartness is all on the surface. A woman was quoted in the papers a day or so after the regatta as saying that she was 'at Ascot last week and it's hideously commercialised. Henley is amazingly English and completely unchanged. I can't remember the last time I saw a foreigner'.

Of course, Henley is seething with foreigners, all rowing the boats: University of Oklahoma Rowing Club, Belgrade RC coxed fours or whatever they are. She must have been blind. What she meant was, she couldn't see a foreigner (or 'wog' as they are still known in the Bridge Bar) who looked common or out of place. The apparent homogeneity of Henley society is a real homogeneity, not a gussied-up homogeneity like Ascot.

The segregation of smart and common is made even plainer the moment you step out of the canvas embrace of Stewards' and walk up the towpath leading to the start of the course. Once out of Stewards', Henley Regatta is a mile-long roughhouse. There are beer tents, smouldering burger stalls, trad jazz bands, funfairs, hooligans hurling themselves off bungee jumps while riding bicycles, acres and acres of people of all castes stripping off and roasting themselves in the sunshine. *Summer Holiday* meets Brueghel the Elder. You couldn't find a clearer demarcation of values: a small quantity of retrophiliac posh, barricaded against a contemporary army of – well, everyone *other*.

And yet something was wrong. It wasn't just me hating the presence of a lot of fat men. It wasn't just the fusty, post-war atmosphere. I tried to puzzle it out as the banker and I hosed down our final Pimm's. He started telling me about an acquaintance of his who'd been having an affair with the au pair. Friend and au pair were at home, fucking in the bedroom, when the wife returned unexpectedly. The au pair jumped off the bed and hid behind the curtains. The wife came in and found her husband nude. 'I came home early,' said the husband. 'Just changing.' Then the wife saw the au pair's feet poking out from under the curtains. She divorced him.

'Never,' said the banker, giving me a considered look, 'get an au pair with big feet.'

'Thanks,' I said.

Let's be sure of one thing: Henley is one of the biggest events of the season: a 'major social occasion', according to my new friend Lady Celestria Noel. It was a matter of extreme good luck that I managed to get a ticket for the Stewards' Enclosure at all. It's an event which the anarchist sub-grouping Class War tried to wreck back in the 1980s, seeing how crucially it symbolised an oppressive class structure. It's the kind of event that even posh people refer to with an acknowledgement that it takes class dif-ferentiation to such extremes, it's almost a parody of The Divided Society: 'Henley, *wah-wah*,' they say satirically, to show how unpre-tentious they really are.

But at the same time, I looked at the mob in Stewards' and found myself wondering in what sense they were really at the top of the social ziggurat.

Was it the noise? Instead of the Ascot swell of well-bred rub-bish, the air was filled with something more loutish: more like a huge, open-air version of the din you get in wine-bars in the City of London after work, a rebarbative, masculine churning noise, the sort of noise made – understandably enough – by thick-witted, strapping men who've been in the sun too long and have made inroads into their second gallon of Pimm's.

Was it, alternatively, the hint of meritocracy in the way that members of Stewards' and the Leander Club are elected? If you can row, then you can be a part of Henley even if you didn't go to Eton or Radley. You can row for the police if you absolutely have to, and be part of their rowing squad. Henley-going rowers are not quintessentially upper crust; nor need their friends be.

Was it a piece of mere circular thinking on my part? Because I got into it, it therefore couldn't be posh? Was it the fact that – like at Ascot, or at any sort of big binge these days – the Henley organisers want your money, they want the corporate hospitality tents, they know perfectly well the whole thing cannot be supported by a tiny handful of layabout aristos and so the social tone has to be compromised by the miasma of bums and *arrivistes* who get in because there's no way to stop them?

Or was it that there weren't any horses?

Horses are a drag. They smell, they bite, they kick, they crap everywhere, they're hugely and pointlessly costly. Why bother with a horse when you can have a bicycle? The best way to encounter a horse, as far as I am concerned, is in the Belgian manner – that is, on a warmed plate, surrounded by *frites* and with a little natural gravy. But being posh means having a fondness for these animals; more than a fondness, an identification with them. Horses are – and let's not mince words here – objective correlatives for the condition of poshness.

Think about it: what are the characteristics of a good horse? It should have breeding; it should have character; it should be a good sort, without too much evident malice; it should enjoy outdoor pursuits; it should be bright enough without actually being an intellectual (you don't want the damn thing sitting down and reading Gérard de Nerval instead of getting out after a fox); it should be clearly expensive to run without being entirely pauperising. Dogs, of course, fulfil these criteria as well, which is why they're also central to posh culture. But they don't fulfil them with quite the same presence, on the same scale, as horses. They're not defining in quite the same way.

You can sense the *frisson* of horseflesh the moment you turn up at a big race, or at a polo game, or even at such nitwit encounters as the Burghley Horse Trials or the Tattersall's Horse Sales. Admittedly the *frisson* is pretty well buried at the Burghley Horse Trials, but it emerges eventually, if you persevere.

Initially I had high hopes of the Burghley Trials – course laid out by Captain Mark Phillips, Burghley House (1552) looming like a film set in the background - but when I got there I found the whole thing dominated by a huge city of trade stalls with names like Over the Top Textiles, Dozydog Petbeds, the Yoghurt Shoppe and the World Famous Joke Shop (this last selling Fart Gas, Shit In A Can and Dr Goodwind's Fart Powder). In a pen next to the car park, a madman was running the Pedigree Chum Fun Dog Agility Trials. He shouted into his microphone, 'The goody bag has all sorts of things, including – what, George? – a pooper-scooper! What George calls a collectors' item!' The Queen wasn't there. It was asinine.

And yet the presence of horses (doing dressage on the day I went; an event in which you watch turn-of-the-century shop window dummies trotting) still gave it a magic, a spiritual lift. It brought out just enough of *those* people: red-faced men with wrecked teeth and yellow corduroy trousers; middle-aged women in navy blazers and Alice bands, faces like well-bred dogs. They stalked the grounds purposefully, looking for worm pills and easy-action cast-iron stoves and so on. And they could have been transposed to Royal Ascot without turning a hair. Even an old county type whom I caught berating her Jack Russell ('Jake! You'll sit down when I tell you and not when you feel like it!') could have been cleaned up and sent into the Royal Enclosure.

And I could sense the mystical, symbolic power of the horse even more powerfully at the next Big Thing in my season: a polo game I went to at Cowdray Park, in West Sussex, shortly after the Henley job.

Cowdray Park is big-time in polo terms, not because it's physically very impressive, but because it occupies such a prominent space in the consciousness of horse-minded posh people. Certainly, the Guards Polo Club at Windsor has the more financially burnished events of the season (the Alfred Dunhill Queen's Cup; the Cartier International Polo Day, where you can feast on visiting guests such as Rod Stewart and Claudia Schiffer); and there are viable polo grounds near Cirencester and Winkfield. But Cowdray does seem to take it terribly seriously, running a bustling calendar of fixtures from April to September, rather than occasional, sponsor-laden one-offs, in the manner of the Guards Club. Names like the Jersey Lilies Cup and the Tyro Cup and the Prince Philip Trophy and the Gold Cup feature prominently in its schedules. It is clearly for horse-mad diehards, rather than fleeting celebs – which is why I bent my efforts there, rather than anywhere more obviously lustrous.

Cowdray Park actually seems to consist of several different grounds to play on, all calling themselves Cowdray Park and all spread indiscriminately around a mass of tiny country lanes in the Midhurst region. This means that despite the breezy promotional crap that Cowdray has started to produce in order to entrap middle-class conies into watching a polo game ('Combine a day out in the beautiful Sussex countryside with the opportunity to enjoy the Sport of Kings'), getting there turns out to be such a pointlessly esoteric business that you wonder why they even bother to advertise.

So I found myself driving endlessly around fields of beet and nameless vegetable growths one weekday afternoon, searching for the semi-finals of the Holden White Cup and the Ruins Cup (named after the sixteenth-century Cowdray Ruins, which may have been near where the event was taking place). The sun was shining and the air was blue with dust and pesticides. Every now and then I would spot a jaunty yellow marker, jammed in a hedgerow or tied to a fingerpost, reading POLO. I'd dive off down a lane to emerge at some deserted rural crossroads, with no sign of POLO or anything else, except more hectares of sugar beet or set-aside.

I began to get a little hysterical, in a sleepy, bucolic way, and was genuinely wondering if I would ever get out of West Sussex, let alone see a polo game. Then I crested a small hill and found the game at my feet.

In the mild delirium of the lanes and hedgerows, I'd begun to picture my first polo ground as a something like a mediaeval jousting arena, full of pennons and oriflammes. I had imagined groupings of little tents, frilled and bedecked with heraldic symbols. I had imagined prancing horses, caparisoned with fine cloth-of-gold and velvet.

What I actually found was an extremely large, empty field, with a huge orange clock (sponsored by a firm of chartered surveyors) on wheels on one side of it and a very small tent (for refreshments) on the other side. Next to the refreshment tent stood an equally tiny open grandstand, about the size and shape of the grandstands you used to buy as accessories for your Scalextric set back in the 1960s.

A tall, thin man wearing a straw hat with an immense brim sold me a ticket at the entrance to the field in what struck me as a mildly surreal manner, and I drove across the landscape to where a couple of other cars had lined up on the edge of the ground. I parked next to a Swiss couple staring at a touring map of southern England. After a while, they put down the map and together we watched the first chukka of polo in uncomprehending silence.

If ever a sport demanded the label *posh*, polo is that sport. Originating 2,500 years ago somewhere in the East, polo was first played at international level between the Iranians and the Touranians, around 600 AD. It arrived in England in 1869 when an officer in the 10th Hussars called 'Chicken' Hartopp read about it in a copy of *The Field*. He is supposed to have cried out, 'By Jove, this must be a good game,' after reading *The Field*'s description of an Indian game called 'hockey on horseback'. Hartopp and the rest of the fellows at once went out and attempted it, eight a side, using chargers and a billiard ball. By 1875, the rules of the game had been formalised by the Hurlingham Club (whose polo grounds, I was pleased to discover, were compulsorily purchased by the London County Council after the Second World War) and now, a century or so later, 'Competition,' according to my Cowdray programme, 'is increasing at all levels of the game.' The programme also pointed out on page 25 that 'British Airways have kindly transported all the polo balls from Dallas, Texas,' for no clear reason.

The rules of polo look simple enough, written down, but when the teams (four horsemen on each side, unlike 'Chicken' Hartopp's demented eight) actually got going, it looked much less like a game and much more like an ill-planned skirmish from some forgotten war. Everyone charged in all directions, cursing with astonishing violence.

'Fuck it!' shouted one of the players, about fifty yards away.

'Jesus Christ!' shouted another player, and pretty soon they were all at it. The next thirty seconds passed like this:

'Bloody hell!'

'Fuck it!'

'Fucking hell!'

'Shit! Shit!'

I suppose I was both ingenuous and literal-minded to assume (as I did) that, since polo was an aristocrat of sports, a sport of kings, a sport, let's face it, played by Cream's old drummer, Ginger Baker, that if there was going to be any sound beyond the thwack of ball and stick, it would be like something out of an old Western Brothers routine – after you, Kenneth, no after *you*, George – that kind of thing. This cascade of, well, *filth*, was unnerving.

Every now and then a bell would ring and the two teams would stop screaming and regroup in the centre of the ground or wander off in a lazily purposeful fashion to the edge of the field. Then the play and the obscenities would start again. Insofar as I understood what was going on, I thought I was watching a team called Kingsmead playing a team called Lambourne. Lambourne had one player called Marin-Mareno and another called Puaca. I wondered if these men had anything to do with the mysterious Gaucho figures driving beaten-up Golf GTis around the perimeter of the ground, along a track which bore notices reading SLOW BECAUSE OF DUST.

Now and then the ball would shoot off the ground altogether, to be retrieved by one of the twenty or so spectators watching from the relative safety of the car park. A dread began to form within me, the kind of dread I used to experience when forced to play cricket at school: the kind of dread I used to feel when being made to field, standing as far away from the action as I could, praying that the ball wouldn't come my way. I could picture the damn thing rolling to a halt between my ankles and some frothing Hooray on a horse shouting at me to throw the ball back. And I could picture myself doing my usual spavined lob so that the ball ended up a mere ten feet away from where I stood, and all the other Hoorays bellowing *JENNINGS!* at me, the way it used to be in the fifth form.

I got so paranoid at the thought of this that I actually climbed back into my car to hide. I then made a great show of studying the programme, pursing my lips ruminatively, screwing up my eyes at the small print and generally going through an entire pantomime of expressions, in order not to look like a man hiding in his car from the game he'd specifically come to watch.

But the chukka soon came to an end, and the Swiss couple next to me got into their car, opened up the touring map and drove away, shaking their heads. Very slowly, people who'd been sitting on the far side of the pitch – those in the nobs' enclosures, in fact – began to amble across the grass, stamping in a deliberate manner on the ground. After a while there were about twenty-five of them, circling and re-circling the turf. They were staring at their feet and bringing their heels down with the sort of angry vigour you would use to stamp on a wasp. This was divot time: something I'd been told about by a bloke who claimed to have gone out on to the polo ground at Windsor to stamp a divot and found himself next to the Queen (headscarf, Hanoverian frown), also stamping on divots. 'Treading in' is the technical name. An idiot's version of grape-pressing.

Something about this must have made me feel that perhaps I wasn't going to be beaten up after all – the spectacle of a lot of county people behaving ludicrously, I suppose – so I braced myself and started to walk from the car-park side of the ground to the smart side, the side with the tent and the microstand. It was a warm, breezy sort of afternoon, a real high-summer afternoon, in fact, and I had to walk about a quarter of a mile to get from my car round the end of the ground to the tent.

I scuffed my way over the grass, drifting into a generalised daydream. I could see the rustic scoreboard in the far corner (angled so that the nobs could read it, but not the bums in the car park), and I admired the sweep of the fields and hills in the blue distance. It was typical, English stuff, domestic in scale, understated, gentle. And it was only after my daydream had really started to take hold and dissolve into semi-consciousness that the men on horses attacked me.

To put it another way, there I was, a solitary slouching figure on the margin of the field, making my way slowly towards a distant patch of beets, when eight large people astride eight hysterical horses came thundering towards me, screaming abuse. It was terrifying. I felt like a footsoldier trudging away from the scene of a disastrous battle, only to be set upon by a delinquent squadron of the enemy's cavalry.

Suddenly I was in a pure, panic-stricken, class confrontation: plodding villein overpowered by shrieking knights. What's more, they were rich shrieking knights – or at least, rich by association, since a team of polo ponies costs upwards of £400,000 a season to run (the term 'pony' is, incidentally, typical class mendacity. These creature are huge and barely tamed). Wealth and privilege were crashing towards a disenfranchised me, as if 600 years of social and constitutional reform had just gone out of the window and all that could save me would be the intercession of St Maurice of Agaunum, the patron saint of infantrymen. Hundreds of thousands of pounds of horse and rider shook the ground, shouting *fuck fuck fuck fuck* and making the dust boil up from their hooves. I toyed with the idea of dropping to my knees and begging them not to disembowel me because of my middle-class clothes and my clear horror of smart physical activity. But instead I tried to break into a discreet run, doing my best to make it look as if I had urgent business in the tent, or needed to quiz the two languid teenagers manning the scoreboard about some point of procedure. But I couldn't manage that either. I slowed breathlessly to a halt and waited for them to butcher me.

Then I saw the ball. I realised that it wasn't me they were after, but the ball. This just gave me time to dread again that I might have to pick it up and throw it to one of the players, but then someone collected it with his stick, turned it and his horse round, and started to pound off in a different direction. 'A player may ride an opponent off,' it said in the rules, 'but must not charge at an angle.' I wondered what would have happened to me if one of them had tried to charge the other one off at the point where I was standing. The thought made my vision blur, so I did my best to put some more ground between me and the psychopaths and get to the refreshment tent.

Having finally inched my way around the field and drawn level with the microstand, it became clear that the smart side of the ground was full of the players' friends and relations. An old lady was sitting in a little enclosure with a wooden paling round it. She held an Edwardian parasol, the sort with tassles dangling from the rim, in her hand and said, 'Oh, Benjy, *Benjy*,' in a bitter tone of voice as the game rolled on. Then there was a bit more yowling from the players, the game was over, and everyone started cantering off the ground and dismounting.

One of the psychos had scored a goal, and this elicited a lot of pawing and slapping from a big fellow in the microstand, who said to the scorer, 'You ought to be very proud of that goal! Heck of a goal! That's the sort of goal the old man used to steal!'

The player wiped his sweaty face and made a few token *hur hurs* of resistance. Another player was being mauled by a big blonde Arabella type, who waggled his elbow and shouted to her friends,

'Hello! Here you are! The hero of the hour! Did they hit you in the balls? Ha, ha, ha, ha!'

I marched thirstily up to the refreshment tent, my change jingling in my pocket. I could glimpse the rear of the bar, through a flap in the canvas. I could see tea, beer, spirits. There were shining cups and glasses and counters and people in white shirts whose job it was to fill these things with drink.

And I was not allowed in. To get in, I had to go through an entrance in the little wooden paling (where the old bag who knew Benjy sat), and the little wooden paling denoted the Members' Enclosure. NO ADMISSION WITHOUT BADGES, it said. I didn't have a badge, so I couldn't go in.

I couldn't believe it. I had risked my neck, my sanity, dragging myself round the ground – indeed, I had fried my brains for half an hour in a traffic jam on the A3 a little earlier – only to find that some prick thought it worth going to the trouble of excluding me and my money from the beer tent simply because I wasn't a member. What was the *point*? There couldn't have been more than seventy of us cretins watching this preposterous spectacle on an abandoned field in the middle of West Sussex. We were all in it together: for whatever perverse reasons, we had all made the effort. In fact we were doing Cowdray Park a favour by bothering to turn up at all. Let's face it, it was hardly a magnet for the well-heeled and discerning. It wasn't Pavarotti at La fucking Scala. And yet someone still thought it both meaningful and necessary, in this home counties dustbowl, to draw a line between members and commoners, between the smart set and the rest of the world.

I stood at the entrance to the members' world, too stupid with rage to know what to do next. The woman with the parasol was now busy having an evidently chewy conversation with an old fart in the chair next to her. She had a drink in her hand.

I couldn't think of anything to do except walk all the way back to my car, in the dust, champing at my gums. I stared at an unusually filthy black Golf GTi parked in one of the reserved parking places, its passenger seat crowded with polo sticks, and wondered whether or not to kick it. Being middle class, I didn't of course. I just savoured my bile and felt aggressively sorry for myself. Then I started off round the edge of the ground again.

By this time, I was past caring whether or not the Hoorays ran me down. In fact, I tried to shut out the racket from the field – 'Sweet Jesus' – 'Your line, Alex, your line!' – and concentrate on getting to my car and going home. After a while, though, I realised that one of the players was being sedulously hacked by an opponent. I paused to watch them. The bloke being hacked stopped his horse, got off and started to hobble around, clutching his leg.

'Jesus Christ!' he shouted. 'Look what you bloody did!'

The guilty party hauled at his reins and his horse slowed to a rabid, twitching pause.

'I've got every right to!' he shouted back at the bloke on the ground.

'You just came up the back!' said the first one.

'Oh, stop being such a bloody disgrace!' said the second one.

This went on for several minutes. The other players ambled up and down, plucking at their sleeves and adjusting their helmets and no one seemed particularly bothered. I guessed that this kind of senseless acrimony must be all part of the game, like the Tourette's syndrome swearing. The two well-bred voices followed me round the edge of the field, barking in the stillness like a couple of dogs after a tennis ball. Finally the injured rider got back on his horse and the game carried on. I climbed sweatily back into my car and got lost again among the interminable hedgerows.

That's what was missing from Henley: all that violence, that class horror, that mediaeval brutality, those squandered millions. Without horses, the whole thing seems somehow prosaic, saddened. I mean, what could be more pitiful, more tragic, even, than the sight of some poor solitary bastard killing himself in a rowing boat, his face purple, the perspiration dripping from his cheeks, the indifference of the drunken crowd (full of fatuous lawyers and accountants) emphasising his isolation?

You don't get that with horses. You get the knightly class, thrashing around on a great panting extension of themselves, disdaining the world. Look at the heaving oarsmen: they're like small businessmen, fighting against a tide of overdue payments and punitive overdrafts as they shoulder their way upriver. Look at the polo players: filthy and grunting and cursing, but still masters of their moronic, evil-tempered horses. And still six feet up in the air, their knees the height of our noses. You can see why smart people like being around them. You can see why they might appeal to the Queen.

And of course, it points up the fact that smart people like to *do* things. They must do things to be who they are. Once you've got the voice, once you've got all that mental garbage in place, once you've got the look, you must go out and do something with it. Inactivity, contemplation and inertia are middle-class practices. A middle-class person can do any number of things (other than the things that posh people do) or do nothing at all, without compromising the quiddity of his or her middle-classness. But a posh person must do certain things, on a regular basis, so as not to lapse from the caste.

And who, frankly, goes out *rowing*?

FIVE

What the socially smart purport to do is their duty. Duty is a strange, mobile concept, which seems to be central to the posh life, but which, typically enough, makes almost no sense when viewed from a literal-minded, bourgeois standpoint. Duty can be a charity gift fair, a sense of history, an army geezer cutting a bit of red tape, some toff thinking about his trees, or it can be an evening of wanton, fatheaded profligacy just off Park Lane.

Why duty? Why now? What got me thinking about it was the last item on that list: that deb's playground, Queen Charlotte's Ball, on 25 September at the Grosvenor House, Park Lane, for which I rashly bought two tickets. 'A major part of the traditional season,' said the guide. I bought myself a rather nice Tony Bennett-style dinner jacket from Marks & Spencer, plus a do-it-yourself bow tie with full instructions. I kept these instructions in an inside pocket at all times, because I knew that if my tie came undone, I would be unable to do it up again without the full six-step procedure and a mirror. I then forced my wife to overcome her natural repugnance for such events and loaded her into a becoming multi-coloured ballgown. Three hours after getting dressed and in a swamp of unease, we piled through the main doors of the Grosvenor House ballroom in Park Lane, past a skimpy retinue of flunkeys and down into the arena where the ball was to take place.

By now, the season – those open-air things which habitually take place in high summer – had mutated into something more indoorsy called the 'little season'. Everyone goes away in August, (to somewhere hot, like Barbados or Greece; or to Scotland, to kill things on the Glorious Twelfth) and then starts to come back to London and the home counties in September. And of all the residual events of the 'little season', Queen Charlotte's Ball is the only one which still harks back to the formal calendar of the debutante's year. It's the last cry of that vanished world.

Having made our way down a mirrored staircase to the ball-room entrance, we found, as promised, hundreds of young women, hurrying apprehensively to and fro and puffing on gaspers to steady their nerves. There were also a surprisingly large number of young men in full white tie and tails. The invitation (£90 a head) actually said White Tie Preferred but, quite apart from the expense, I hadn't wanted to walk around dressed like a variety show conjuror. Still. The young gentlemen weren't bothered. There were even some full-dress oldsters who'd gone to the trouble of putting Iron Crosses round their necks and pinning other bits of militaria to themselves. I saw a sort of fall of the House of Romanov dowager princess – quite old, Warhol-white skin, crown of black hair, tiara, expression of ossified disdain – being squired by an old boy done up as Peter Ustinov in period gear: plenty of ribbons and sashes. It was all rather lovely, like a painting by Tissot, or William Quiller Orchardson.

We had to get our table number at a desk staffed by some

aristocratic young ladies. There we found that Mr and Mrs Jennings had actually been allocated four places spread over two tables: number 64 and number 42. 'Oh dear,' said an aristo, fiddling with the documents I'd damply proffered her. 'Well, which one would you like?' Since number 64 was on the outer reaches of the seating arrangements, somewhere near Goods Access, we went for 42, right in the thick of things. Grinning with nerves, we then went in past a dismayed-looking Lesley Joseph out of *Birds of a Feather*, who was doing a broadcast for L!VE TV.

The Grosvenor House ballroom (actually called the Great Room) is basically a large interior space about the size of a football pitch, surrounded by a gallery and done up in a glum, sub-French empire style. Lutyens designed the exterior, but you wouldn't know it once inside. The predominant tones are old gilt and mud, while at one end, an overweening double staircase leads from the floor to the gallery. Being big and stodgy in appearance, the Great Room actually has rather a town-hall atmosphere to it. My guess is that when empty, it smells of gravy and vests. According to the woman who organised charity balls and knew how many generations of schooling it took to transform your children into elitists, it is nevertheless *the* London venue for any ball with pretensions: to the extent that, if your ball does not take place at Grosvenor House, there has to be a reason why not.

For the purposes of the Queen Charlotte's Birthday Ball, to give it its full title, a well-punished bandstand and dancefloor had been set out at the other end from the staircase, while a huge closed-circuit TV screen had been hung up on a wall. There were a multitude of helium balloons about, some coloured spotlights, a lot of circular tables for the guests to eat at, and a parade of cut-out cardboard 1960s mannequin shapes – 2D Jean Shrimptons – fixed all around the gallery. Each lady guest got a bottle (about the size of a gooseberry) of Penhaligon's scent, and a lacy hanky courtesy of the White House of Bond Street. Champagne was by Palmer and the decoration design by Harvey Nichols. And there was a cake, a simply vast cake, rendered in adamantine white icing, standing on the dancefloor, with a gas jet burning at its crown. It looked like something from Mussolini's Rome.

Table 42, it turned out, was being hosted by a startling middle-aged woman with beehive blonde hair and a blue gown shaped like a satin ice-cream cone from which she emerged as a piece of living confectionery at the top. '*Hello!*' she cried, stretching out her gloved hand. 'I'm Sally! And who are *you*?'

I just about managed to get our names out before she threw herself into a torrential account of why, exactly, we were on her table and not someone else's. Not, for example, on table 64, by the tradesmen's entrance. She'd been let down, you see. She'd got her table of ten meticulously together, months in advance, and then one of her couples had dropped out.

'Of course, I was on the phone to the chairman of the com-mittee, saying, for heaven's sake, don't give us someone old and boring and stuffy, and she said, Sally, it's for *charity*, and of course she was quite right, but you and your wife look absolutely delightful anyway! Ha, ha, ha, ha!'

Then Sally set about introducing us to the other people at her table, who were standing around talking guardedly to each other. There was a dark-haired boy – twenty-six, maybe – next to her. He wore white tie and tails and smoked a long cigarette.

'This is Paul,' she screamed, 'his father owns half of Norway.'

Paul stepped forward and did some hand-shaking. By this stage I felt both eerily detached from events and, at the same time, enmeshed in something uncontrollable and vaguely threatening. Paul's face was like the face of a movie star, sharp-edged, framed by thick black hair, slightly sinister, held with the sort of rigid poise that obliged him to peer down his nose at us, and us to peer beseechingly back up at him.

'Do you like films?' he said.

I grunted at him.

'Did you like *Pulp Fiction*?' he went on.

He didn't wait for me to say that I hadn't got round to it, and indeed, was still saving up for *Reservoir Dogs*, before he nailed the subject into its coffin. '*Pulp Fiction*,' he informed me, 'is immoral. All that killing. I prefer love. That is not immoral.'

I turned blankly away to look at the other guests. On the opposite side of the table were a newly married couple – under thirty, like Paul – who'd just come back from a spell in Hong Kong, where he'd been an investment banker and she'd been something in retailing. There was also a lugubrious shop-designer who spent the whole evening trying to go to sleep in his chair, plus Paul's normal-looking girlfriend. And there was a man with a big nose and a woman in a red ballgown, to whom I did not address a single word all night. And that made up our table. I wondered whether or not to retch into the complimentary lace hanky, but my mind was made up for me when some big cheese on the top table told us all to shut up and say Grace.

Had this been just any old ball, an event with no greater meaning – some Hooray's birthday party, or something – then I would have grasped the point more readily. But there were various subtexts running through the encounter which gave it a sense of confusion all of its own.

The first point to remember was that it was duty. Sally and her friends were doing this for *charity*, to help maintain and support the Queen Charlotte's Maternity Hospital. The intense ballgowns, the white ties, the screaming, the luscious perfumes, the heavy-lidded insolence were all in a good cause.

For the middle classes (it goes without saying), duty means suffering. It's one of those bourgeois pieties: to do good it has to be painful. The barely latent puritanism of the middle classes means that charity is mortifying. Visiting Gran in the bin, running an unfeasible gift stall, forgoing a punt on the lottery in order to give your last pound coin to the blind dogs woman: you have to deny yourself in some way. The very idea of demonstrating your sense of duty by going out and eating and drinking and dancing and shouting at your friends simply does not make sense. How was Sally suffering? How was she *giving*, except insofar as she had to spend an evening sitting next to me (harrowing enough, I'll grant you) instead of the person she'd originally planned to sit next to? Don't tell me she was making a financial sacrifice. She looked as costly and as manually perfected as the Rolls–Royces in the showrooms round the corner in Berkeley Square.

It's hard for people like me to understand, but Queen Charlotte's Ball has always managed to conflate the idea of charity with the idea of a lot of over-privileged people having limitless fun. The first ball was held as a hospital fund-raiser in 1928, along with a swimathon (prizes given out by Tallulah Bankhead) and guest appearances by Jessie Matthews and Sophie Tucker. Then, the cake was cut by the Duchess of Argyll, the great-granddaughter of the original Queen Charlotte, who had become patron of the first maternity hospital in 1809. Rapidly establishing itself as a high point in the debutante's year, it reached some kind of peak in 1940, when Winston Churchill took his daughter along. In 1958, the ball became a semi-official function after presentations at court came to an end, and in 1960, more than 350 debs took part, all bowing to the big cake instead of to the Queen. Two generations ago, in other words, Queen Charlotte was really something. Nothing to do with self-denial and not much, at an individual level, to do with the mitigation of suffering or injustice: just a quality bash.

By 1976, I have to point out, the original sequence of balls had come to a sordid end. The anarchic dismemberment of the post-war consensus which was the seventies saw Queen Charlotte's collapse into a farrago of gatecrashers, streakers and mulish young women who didn't want to be debs in the first place. But then Bunty Lewis singlehandedly resuscitated it for the hospital's 250th anniversary, back in 1989; and – showing unusual tenacity – it seems to have dragged on, year after year, up to the moment when I arrived. Bunty's good fortune, you see, was to discover a new generation of young women prepared to act as debs in a spirit of candid irony: thus it was revived, true to its principles of extreme selfishness in aid of something vaguely benign. Which is what I don't understand. It's like making National Asthma Week an opportunity for sponsored wine-tastings. Or holding a rout for Help the Aged at Stringfellow's.

However – and this is the second point at which I lose touch with the concept of Queen Charlotte's – there was controversy. The year we went, Queen Charlotte's Ball was disappearing under bad press because the organiser, Mrs Lewis, had been in a fight with a man called Peter Townend. Peter Townend has, apparently, been Mr Season for years, acting as a coming-out party-arranger for young debs and an arbiter of who should meet whom on the smart social scene. 'A man with green teeth,' is how one person described him. He got pissed off with Bunty because Bunty was taking the ball downmarket and letting all sorts of social detritus (people like me) attend, and not maintaining the highest standards of snobbery set in the days when the ball was a lodestar in the debs' calendar. She had, in fact, let it become nothing more than a blatant dodge for raising cash for an institution which the Department of Health ought to have supported. Obviously, in a good and fair world, hospitals would be funded centrally by money raised through taxation. But because we live in a society largely organised by venal morons, the principles of fair taxation and redistribution don't work. But then, I don't think that was what was bothering Peter Townend. Indeed, he seemed to have forgotten entirely that charity was the thing that brought the ball into existence – fair enough, if you look at the event cynically – and was mainly concerned with the fact that, being a gathering of rich, witless, upper-class wastrels, it deserved something better than commoners from the outer suburbs. Or foreigners.

Because the crisis hinged on this: Mrs Lewis had let in some American girls (from Fort Lauderdale) as debs, with full accreditation, white ballgowns, curtseying and so on. These Americans were really too much for Mr Townend, who decided to boycott the event. The American girls went back to Fort Lauderdale in disgust, Mrs Lewis was outraged and the row between Peter and Bunty drew the kind of attention which would have embarrassed a dog-track consortium, let alone London's premier ball. The issue was lobbed around by the yellow press, who denounced the event as a social obscenity, while others stuck up for it as a bit of harmless fun. 'Those who jeer,' pronounced *Tatler*, 'are suffering from a sense-of-humour failure.'

But what kind of mental universe was Peter Townend inhabiting when the row blew up? Queen Charlotte's Hospital is just a hospital. It's not the Throne Room of Buckingham Palace. It doesn't reek of immemorial grandeur – indeed, the flinty-hearted Hammersmith and Hounslow Health Authority were, at the time of writing, talking about closing it down and merging it with the Hammersmith Hospital. It's a utility. How could anyone get from this fundamental reality to a position so extreme, so hypercritical, that they could object to the presence – to the *idea* – of two pretty, well-bred girls from Florida?

After Grace (led by guest star the Duchess of Somerset), a load of food turned up on our plates, served with furious concentration by an army of lackeys. At flash, heavily catered events, the food usually looks better in French than it does on the plate. Thus, Queen Charlotte's *suprême de pintade poêlée mascotte* was a small dead bird with gravy, while the *rendez-vous de légumes* was quintessentially just veg. The *sorbet de mangues Reine Charlotte* did have a cameo of Queen Charlotte on the top, but it tasted like soap, as is the way with these things.

But then, I wasn't there for the food. I was there for the people. As we ploughed into our starters (a greasy *mousseline de saumon florentine*), my wife was being quietly numbed by the Hong Kong banker. 'I've just bought a disused church in St John's Wood,' I heard him say. 'I've had to box in my minimalist staircase.' He then asked her if she went to many balls. 'We've stopped going to so many,' he explained. 'They get too boring. Always the same people.' He broke off and called across the table. 'Paul! You're being a shit!' This was delivered with a shrill giggle, as Paul pulled a corner off his bread roll and lobbed it across the table at Mr Hong Kong.

Sally rested her hand on my forearm in a confidential manner. 'Of course, this always happens,' she began. 'I fall in love with my boys and they go and get married. Or they get engaged and then they leave me!' She pawed at Paul, still clutching my arm. 'Don't you, darling!' Paul smirked at her, darkly. I wondered whether or not 'falling in love' with her boys meant having sex with them. She was middle-aged but voluptuous and effervescent to a fault. Her bosom heaved and fell. She wore a wedding ring, plus an engagement ring with a rock of immense size and brilliance, but there was no sign of her husband, nor any mention of him. I tried not to let my puzzled frown show too much, and essayed a couple of jokes to put her at her ease. Unfortunately, she became hysterical.

'Oh! This is wonderful!' She was deafening me. '*Two* jokes! He's a comedian! Paul! Charles is so funny! This is such good news, because when we were told we were going to have to share, well, we were so worried it was going to be someone *boring*!'

I forked in a few hectic mouthfuls of food and tried to think of something unboring to say to her. But she was so determined to make things go with a swing that before I'd really managed to assemble any ideas, I found that she was clutching my arm again and muttering into my ringing ears.

'I've just written,' she said, 'an erotic novel.'

I froze, feeling intensely middle class. What do you say to an hysterical swanky middle-aged woman who's just announced that she's written an erotic novel?

I had no way of coping with this sudden intelligence. It was one thing to be gripped by class paranoia, but something else completely to be gripped by class paranoia, sexual unease *and* conceptual helplessness at the same time.

Fortunately, Sally spotted the fact that I was in trouble and filled the gap herself.

'It's forty-five chapters long,' she explained. I managed a hoarse gasp of surprise, tinged with what I hoped was a rattle of congratulation. 'I haven't found a publisher yet, but my agent's working on it.' Was this why she was surrounded by young men? Research for her erotica? No time to speculate on this, either, because she was off again.

'I know them all, you know,' she went on, 'all the celebrity writers. I could know Julie Burchill if I tried. And they're all so *frightful*.' She took a sip of wine and shook her head. 'You know, I've got a wonderful idea for a column I could write. I could do a profile of a writer each week and *really* let the world know what they're up to. Really turn the tables! Ha, ha, ha, ha, ha!'

She spoke in a breathless, irresistible cascade. The trouble was that her words were coming at me so fast, and meant so little to me, that I couldn't even imagine what sort of general noise I ought to make in response – let alone what specifics I should come up with. Looking back, I suppose the right thing to have done would have been to pat her flirtatiously on the wrist and say something like, 'Sally, how *brilliant*, that would be *so* funny!' And then laugh with a mad gaiety. But frankly, I'd find it easier to swim the Baltic than come up with bright small talk.

I think she must have seen my eyes go blank, because she started tugging at Paul's sleeve.

'Paul! Tell Charles about the time we hijacked that man's car . . .'

Paul shifted around in his seat in a lazy, lubricated sort of way. His gaze fell on me. He seemed to be unsure whether it was even worth his while opening his mouth to talk to me. Perhaps Sally spotted this, because she didn't bother to wait for him to cruise into action. She set off again, at her usual frantic pace.

'We were at this party, and we were rather enjoying ourselves—'

'Drugs?' I blurted out.

'Oh no, not *drugs*.' She gave me a brief look of hatred and then composed herself, her gleaming smile back on her face. 'Champagne and vodka, darling. Champagne and vodka.'

I'm sorry if any of this sounds incredible, but I have not invented a single word of it. In an ideal world, I would have jotted down her thoughts as she spoke, but I had to make do with committing them to memory and then dashing off to the lavatory once she'd finished and writing them in my notebook. There may be an expression or two out of place, an emphasis missed, but otherwise, this is what she said.

'Anyway,' she went on, 'I knew about this really wonderful party on the other side of town and we *had* to get there and we couldn't get a taxi. So we stopped this little man in a Volkswagen and said, "Take us to the other party!"'

I bayed with laughter at her. She acknowledged me, then continued, 'And he took us to the other party! He was *so* sweet. We were all in the back, kissing each other and drinking champagne and using our phones and we said, you *must* come to the party, you've been *so* sweet! And he said, no, he was an accountant and he had to go home and read a book.'

Paul had decided to invest some of his time in us by this point. After I'd summoned up a few *nos!* and *you don't says!* of encouragement to Sally, he took a languorous drag at his cig and said, 'Yes, he was a funny little man. I can't think why he did it.'

Maybe this isn't strange at all. Maybe London is full of people like Sally and Paul and the Hong Kong banker and his wife, all forcing their way into private cars and compelling their owners to drive across town to parties. Maybe the world of *Vile Bodies* never came to an end.

These people were barely intelligible to me. Paul, with his oily indifference; Mr Hong Kong, with his little screams of ecstasy; Mrs Hong Kong, porcelain and frosty; the shop-designer, trying to sleep through it, but jerking out of his chair now and then to stare balefully at someone across the room; the man with the big nose and the red ballgown woman, who by now had tied themselves up in a conversation of limitless complexity; and Sally, sounding like a klaxon. They were so much like characters out of Waugh that I didn't see how they could even exist in the world as I understood it. They were posturing, sniggering, preening posh. I felt that not only could I not understand them, they couldn't understand me either. Your conventional Sloane would at least know what I was, even if he thought I ought to be used for hare-coursing. But with these people, I felt like something left behind on a Petri dish.

★

But was this even a ball? Or was it what my parents' generation would have called a 'dinner dance'? I thought a ball was something where an orchestra played in a great room which gave on to smaller rooms, where you could eat and drink and intrigue. And there would be a terrace; yes, a terrace where you would step out into the moonlight and the scent of the stocks and clinch your lover, before tottering back inside and sucking down booze until dawn. Whatever pretensions the Grosvenor House Great Room may have had, I realised it wasn't going to be quite that way. But did it have to be quite so blatant?

Some time before, you see, I'd been to a Scottish dancing class at Wandsworth Town Hall. It made a pointed comparison; and it required me (something I was naturally keen to avoid) to arbitrate between two distinct versions of poshness.

Consider Scottish dancing. Like Queen Charlotte's Ball, it requires space, time and money to get right; like Queen Charlotte's, it's been given the royal seal of approval (the Queen Mother had written a fleeting dedication in the ball programme: 'I hope that everyone at Grosvenor House this evening will enjoy the ball', while Princess Margaret is regularly pictured in the glossies throwing shapes during the Scottish-dancing season); it's also necessarily highly social; it's snobbish; and when all is said and done, it's both an arcane and a stupid thing to do. '*Such* good fun!' say the Sloanes I've asked about it.

The great difference is that whereas anyone could go to Queen Charlotte's, an event utterly lacking in discrimination, almost no one can manage Scottish dancing. It is both elitist and barbarous. The class I visited was run by a terrific Old Etonian called Harry, with a kilt and a dicky leg. He had about 200 urban Sloanes crashing around the town hall one night, in a mixture of awesome complexity and extreme violence.

When I turned up, there were a lot of new recruits being haled through the basic moves by a permanently outraged young man. There was a Grenadier Guards officer in the mob ('I've got a few things in the offing, and I wanted to get a bit of practice in') and a girl from Cheltenham Ladies' College ('It's easy. You just do the same things over and over again'). This is what they had to do, when they were attempting a dance known as the Duke and Duchess of Edinburgh: Couples 1, 2 and 3, forward and back. Clap. Turn partners. 1st couple figure-of-eight round couples 2 and 3, own sides. Tea-pots (sic), right-handed (1st lady with 2nd couple, 1st man with 3rd couple). 1st couple change places; left-handed teapots. 1st couple turn 1st corners (R.H.), partner (L.H.), 2nd corners (R.H.), cross to own side . . . and so on, for a quarter of an hour, non-stop. 'You can get some quite serious injuries,' confided an old hand, brightly.

After half an hour of collisions, Harry the organiser came stumping through a side door, clapping his hands. 'How many people are having supper?' he shouted over the noise. 'Hands up!' Everyone then went and ate quiche and drank Sainsbury's Portuguese red (included in the all-in ticket price of £11) and the numbers grew. Fiercely jolly women in Alice bands started to appear, accompanied by men wearing city shirts and weekend trousers. The social mix was predictably long on SW bankers and estate agents and short, on, say, minicab drivers. 'We've got half our bridesmaids here tonight,' Harry said. 'This is where I met my wife, Scottish dancing. Actually, she was dancing here when she was pregnant, got knocked over on a Thursday night, and on Saturday she delivered the baby.'

Then they all ran out on to the floor again and crashed into each other in time to the music. A top Scottish reels band had set up onstage and the hard-core reelers were doing about 500 rpm. Everyone was covered in sweat, but no blood actually flowed. The room was an orgy of teeth, hair and corduroy. And it epitomised to me, the quietly sneering rational bourgeois in the corner, nursing his glass of Portuguese red, the upper classes at play: pointless, exclusive, homespun, encrusted with tradition, incomprehensible to the outside world. Much more what I would have called worthy of a ball. There was nothing materially flash about it, nothing explicit like Queen Charlotte's, and it could only have appealed to people who were already inducted into its mysteries – unlike the Grosvenor House event, which would have appealed to anyone who liked evening dress, pretentiousness and very large rooms smelling of gravy. Did this make Harry's dancing, paradoxically, smarter?

Back at the Grosvenor House, the raffle came around. The thing about an evening like Queen Charlotte's Ball is that not only do you fork out ninety pounds per head for the tickets, and give to charity that way, but you also have to pitch in a load of money while you're there. This is in order to win some over-priced piece of garbage in a raffle, which then adds still more to the charity's coffers. I had seen this coming – I don't know how, just a moment of intuition – and had made a doleful stop-off at the cashpoint machine on the way. So I had some readies in my pocket at the point when everybody in the Great Room was being urged to buy a raffle ticket and win, among other things, some Ken and Barbie dolls, two nights at the Novotel, Hammersmith and an East 17 album. But did anyone else at our table have any money? These people who had been to so many balls already they were bored with them? Did they have the notes about them? No, they did not. 'Do you take Amex? Ha, ha, ha, ha, ha, ha!' said Paul, flapping open a costly black wallet in which there was, indeed, nothing but credit cards.

The Hong Kong banker was similarly short. 'Oh, come on, Sally,' he shrilled, 'give us a tenner, darling. Don't be a bitch!' Sally didn't have any cash, either (nowhere to put it in her dainty black evening bag, no bigger than a baby's fist) so, like some kind of out-of-town rube, some suburban hayseed who's just been cozened at a game of cards, I ended up putting twenty quid (for the whole table, you understand) into an envelope. I handed it with a cheerless smile to one of the hustlers who was working the floor and collecting the bets. Mrs Hong Kong subsequently won a silver picture frame. I don't know how.

Then Bunty Lewis made her speech to the 1,000-strong mob, many of whom were still grappling with their puddings.

Among all the thank yous and grateful welcomings, she pointedly gave a big hand to 'our friends from the United States'. The girls from Florida must have been prevailed upon to come back. A glance at the programme confirmed this. One page bore an advert from a flash yacht-builders based in Fort Lauderdale ('Proud to Support Queen Charlotte's Hospital' from a distance of 5,000 miles), while the following page had pictures of the two pretty American debutantes themselves, plus quotations from Keats ('Beauty is truth') and Unknown ('Sleep is the effort to throw off moral reform').

Bunty then went on to point out that 'tonight's theme is *A Star is Born*', and gestured towards the ceiling, from which a galaxy of cardboard stars dangled. Finally, she thanked the Duchess of Somerset, and hustled the chef who'd made the cake onstage. He turned out to be a black guy in a chef's stovepipe hat. He stared for about ten seconds into a sea of largely hostile, racist white eyes with a look of terror on his face. Then he ran off again, to a ripple of puzzled applause.

And then the debutantes came in. The air was filled with the sound of Handel's 'Judas Maccabeus', played by the Dark Blues, a super-competent covers band, led by a man who looked like the chairman of a merchant bank. Everyone sat back and lit up a cig.

This was the moment when high society gazed upon itself and approved.

There were thirty-four debs, all done up in large, foamy white dresses. Up to the moment when 'Judas Maccabeus' began, they had all been pacing up and down on the gallery, pinning and combing and tucking themselves for the last time before it was too late. They had also been smoking prodigiously, like snooker players. Then the music started, they put out their fags and tiptoed down the double staircase and along the central aisle between the tables – watched all the time by a video camera which flashed pictures up on to the big wall screen. They were young (mostly under twenty) and pretty in the way that brides manage to look pretty at their own weddings: the kind of failsafe prettiness that results from spending great sums of money securing the services of top hairdressers and frock-makers. Some of them looked terrified, most of them looked as if they would rather have been somewhere else, and some of them were actually having mild hysterics. They marched up to the far end and bowed to the great cake. Bunty solemnly led the applause. And that was it. Handel ended, the debs started to drift apart like spume on the sea, and from then on, the event began to collapse into a sequence of pleasureless to-ings and fro-ings.

First of all, Sally shot out of her seat next to me with an audible cry of relief and went to sit at the neighbouring table (which, it turned out, she had also organised). Then a very hairy man in an odd mixture of evening clothes (dinner jacket, business shirt and white tie) came and took her place.

'This isn't my kind of thing at all, to be honest,' he said, wearily helping himself to a glass of wine. 'I don't know what I'm doing here.' I pulled a face as the Dark Blues launched themselves into their first set of the evening.

My wife, who was almost at breaking point as a result of the attentions of the Hong Kong banker, yanked me to my feet and pulled me briskly towards the dancefloor. The trousers of my new dinner jacket were slightly too large, so I skipped and capered behind her, wrenching my waistband upwards with one hand and cramming in my shirt-tails with the other. We staggered through the Charleston, followed by Tina Turner's 'The Best'. My trousers were falling down at a rate of about an inch every thirty seconds, so I had to dance one-handed (with the other permanently on my midriff), instead of performing my usual two-handed Dionysiac mambo.

Paul, the snotty boy who hated *Pulp Fiction*, was dancing too, but not with his girlfriend. To my surprise, he was doing a tango with an exotic broad in a tight blue dress. They were terribly good at it; they must have done it many times before. Where had she come from? Had I made a mistake over the normal-looking girl who was on our table? I could have sworn that she was with him. But perhaps she wasn't. Perhaps he wasn't with anyone.

I wanted to go home, so I went to the lavatory. I passed a knot of debutantes, standing both stupidly and sweetly watching themselves bow to the cake in a replay on the video screen.

In the Gents', two boys in black tie were staring were staring with drunken fascination into the mirror.

'How do you keep your tie straight?' asked one.

The other one said, 'You fire off smoke flares at thirty thousand feet, dive to ten thousand, pull out of the dive and climb twenty thousand feet.'

'That's how you keep your tie straight?'

The boy who fired off smoke flares to keep his tie straight lurched over to the urinal, muttering, 'No one's ever heard of Mons College. No one's *ever* heard of Mons College.' He turned to me as he peed. 'Have *you* ever heard of Mons College?'

He let go of his cock with his right hand, which he extended to me. I shook it nervelessly.

'Hello,' he said. 'Mons College and Trinity, Cambridge. What about you?'

'Stick to the water,' I said, feeling old, and he went back to his pissing.

But remember: these people were doing their duty. In their conservative, individualistic, selfishly well-moneyed way of things, this was how you did your bit for society. No smelly corporatist solutions here. It might be acting as an artist's patron, it might be throwing your house open for some hopeless craft fair, it might be turning up to watch a team of debutantes bow to a cake – the point was that charity and duty are matters of personal action rather than state obligation.

And the scope of duty is enormous. Over here we have Queen Charlotte's Ball, sniggeringly shoring up a disintegrating wing of the NHS. Over there we have the smart person's *noblesse oblige* – conceptual continents away from the ball, but still intimately related. Over there, in fact, we have Lord Cottesloe.

Lord Cottesloe was actually in Buckinghamshire, opening a row of newly built houses for retired servicemen on the edge of a village, when I went to see him. Why was I picking on Cottesloe? Why servicemen? Merely because I was tipped off by someone who knew about it and said, 'If you want *noblesse oblige*, you'll like this.'

So I drove up to Buckinghamshire one searingly hot afternoon a few weeks before Queen Charlotte's Ball. On the way, I spotted a sign announcing the presence of the ANOOPAM MISSION BRAHMAJYOTI, some cultish home counties infestation a couple of miles from the servicemen's houses. A part of the world, I thought to myself, which still takes communities seriously.

I did my best to approach the whole thing in a spirit of fair-minded tolerance. I suppose if you have to commemorate the opening of a row of houses, you might as well have an ex-serviceman and peer of the realm to do it. Soldiers, retired or otherwise, must have an affinity for that kind of thing. *Noblesse oblige* probably goes with soldiering, in much the same way that petty fraud goes with selling used cars. And as an example of the concept of duty made manifest, Cottesloe absolutely fitted the bill. According to the *Country Life* who's who of Lords Lieutenant, the Lord Lieutenant of Bucks got five points out of five for sheer busyness. He averaged 300 official engagements a year, six to eight royal visits and had recently had a meeting with the President of Nigeria in Milton Keynes. This was all on top of his normal job of being a landowner (over 2,000 acres) and being keen on the Territorials.

Indeed, he made the effort to pitch up to this village in Buckinghamshire on a day when I would normally not have bothered to move from a darkened room. It was mid-afternoon, late summer and hotter than Mercury when Cottesloe's car (a dreary blue Vauxhall with a flag on the front) pulled up. A bluff-looking, red-faced geezer with tortoiseshell half-moons sprang out, wearing a proper collar and tie, and charged over to the people hosting the opening, going, 'Hello, marvellous, splendid – Oh! I would have recognised you by your tie! And you by the elephants! Ha, ha!' The voice was there with stentorian correctness, as was the general air of being *up* and positive and not at all nasty or mean-minded. For someone wearing a buttoned-up jacket in eighty-degree temperatures, I thought he was doing a terrific job.

After a moment's shooting the breeze with some local small shots, Cottesloe took a stance by one of the front doors and launched into a nicely modulated but meaningless speech, beginning with the worlds, 'Homelessness is a feature of life in Great Britain today. And I don't think we can blame anyone specifically.'

I wrote this down with elaborate care, pursing my lips and trying to look like an elderly cub reporter. The rest, however, escaped me in the heat and dust. There was a good deal more stuff about homelessness, plus something about the forthcoming VE Day celebrations. I did notice that Lord C. kept referring to the chairman of the committee responsible as 'sir', and that as he got warmer and warmer in the afternoon sun, so his eyebrows beetled more and more, until they were joined together like a length of rope on his face.

At one point, he found he was standing on a manhole cover. 'Oh dear,' he said, briskly stepping to one side. 'I don't like man-hole covers.'

A couple of minutes later, he discovered himself using a sentence with the phrase 'community welfare' in it. 'Oh dear,' he said again. 'I don't like that. That sounds like local-government language to me.'

And then, with a jingle of keys, he was finished and the houses were duly declared open. A knot of about forty interested locals clapped along with the small shots and I clapped too. Then everyone descended on a line of trestle tables for a traditional hot summer afternoon's repast of boiling tea and thick fruit cake. A woman standing next to me murmured to her friend, 'Don't you think it's clever of him, just to take some notes on something he doesn't know anything about, and turn it into a speech?'

Clearly, she knew more than I did, because it never struck me at any point that Cottesloe was anything other than on top of his subject. He didn't say anything interesting, mark you. But what he said, he said with all the unswerving confidence of a man who has studied his material and studied it at length. I was impressed.

After a bit of tea-drinking and cake-wrestling, he made his good-byes, was bundled back into his gloomy blue Vauxhall and sped off, doubtless to another engagement, or to plot the next arrival of the Queen. And I was left to wonder what difference it would have made to the servicemen and their families if their new homes had been opened by, say, the head of the parks department, or Barbara Windsor.

And then my season got completely derailed when I went off to a land agent for a titled family in the home counties – and found myself drawing all sorts of unmanageable conclusions about this duty business.

S<u>ix</u>

The land agent's job, essentially, was to look after the rural possessions of a titled family in the home counties. Meeting him was nothing more than a digression on my part: I should have been at the Blenheim Horse Trials, but I was fretfully sick of horses, and the land agent struck me as a welcome alternative. In fact, the family for whom he worked was not just titled, they owned over six thousand acres of prime Southern England land, plus a vast manorial home, properties in London, smaller houses elsewhere in the country, business interests and so on. The complete grandee array. The land agent himself occupied a kind of semi-feudal post, in which he subsumed his identity in the identity of the family, and became a sort of curator of their responsibilities to the immediate neighbourhood.

A polite but essentially distant fellow called Michael, in a tweed jacket and socially divisive tie, he had to keep the tenants in their country properties happy, make sure the land yields were satisfactory, clear a profit, maintain the drains – generally keep the rural economy ticking over. He had trained at Cirencester Agricultural College ('The three-year rural estate management course,' apparently, 'not the one-year course. That's known as the gin-and-tonic course. For people not quite so . . . academically competent. I think Mark Phillips did it . . .') and after a spell in East Anglia ended up sitting in the pleasant downstairs office of his Georgian combined home and workplace, with dappled sunlight flickering in at the window, talking to me.

Frankly, he reminded me of Mr Andrews from Gainsborough's *Mr and Mrs Andrews*: Englishness as it would like to be remembered. Decent, humane, eighteenth-century, pompous, no extremes, some bulky white clouds sailing slowly across the pale blue heavens, a pheasant starting from the undergrowth, a silent, dusty yard edged by homely stables . . .

But the moment he started speaking, I discovered that whatever else you learn at Cirencester, you certainly get a good grounding in class platitudes. Before I knew it, the clichés were pouring out. For a start, he began by explaining how the estate was run 'paternalistically'.

Oh, really? Enlightened, eh?

'Oh, yes. The village shop' – which was closed, when I rattled past it an hour later, but, from the look of it, principally sold jam and chicken stuffing – 'is heavily subsidised so that people who live and work on the estate don't have to drive miles to get to a supermarket. And we charge half the rent that would normally be paid on a shop like that.'

As if that piece of market-rigging wasn't enough, there was more, as a testimonial to the farsightedness of the Lord of the Manor.

'There's a chap who's worked on the estate for forty-two years. He's retiring soon, and he'll keep his house *rent free*.'

I nodded and pursed my lips. How wise, I agreed. How

thoughtful. How unlike the common perception of grasping or incompetent landowners callously abusing the livelihoods of their tenants (rent rises, sudden redundancies, exploitative work practices) in order to fend off their creditors.

'And you see, the family very much wants to preserve the estate as it is, with its way of life.'

Here it comes, I thought, restlessly awaiting the pay-off.

'They see their role,' said Michael – or Mr Michael, as I imagine he must be known by the peons – 'as a *stewardship*. For future generations. Conservatism with a small c.'

Is this the single biggest difference between toffs and middle-class people? The idea that while the middle classes live in a more or less continuous present, toffs, aristos and posh people live in a bizarre flux of the historical and the contemporary? We look no further back than our parents and no further forward than our kids, and bumble through life in a largely undifferentiated state of here-and-now awareness. But the upper classes see their actions and responsibilities as part of the great tidal movements of historical change and continuity (even when they're behaving like pieces of dreck. Blandford and Bristol spring to mind – curators of their families' right occasionally to give birth to catastrophic wastrels). Is our sense of history gained by reading popular works of non-fiction, while theirs is in the DNA? Is this why posh people don't seem to define themselves through their jobs in any way like the middle classes? Because a job is just a transient something, while posh people have to keep their eyes on the bigger picture, the eternal verities of time and society?

This is the fantasy that Evelyn Waugh – in all other respects, the greatest English comic novelist of the century – falls for in *Brideshead Revisited*. This is the animating faith of *Country Life* magazine. That they have this indivisible sense of heritage, and we don't.

Perversely enough, even as Mr Michael said the word 'stewardship' (one of those Prince Charles words, stewardship: the lexicon of top-quality homespun crap), I wanted to believe him. There he was in his Georgian house. There was the farmland and the woodland just outside his window, as, presumably, it had been all this century and the century before. There were the old, leather-bound volumes of estate business, resting serenely on a shelf: great ledgers with the names DAY BOOK and ESTATE BOOK embossed on their spines. There, indeed, was a map of the estate, drawn in 1850, and, as he was quick to point out, still remarkably similar to contemporary estate maps. Only a road here and a boundary change there had altered in 150 years. It was all so plausible.

But then he really got into his stride on the subject of the Lord of the Manor's birthday party. When he celebrated his sixtieth birthday, he 'invited all the estate people and their families to the house to celebrate'.

Now, this is meat and drink to apologists for the peerage. This recalls the great revels thrown by people like the Duke of Northumberland in the nineteenth century, with garland-decked tents in the back garden and hundreds of estate workers toasting the master with commemoration ale. Paternalism as socio-economic truth. What's more, 'When the Earl and his wife had their fiftieth wedding anniversary,' said Mr Michael in a heartfelt way, 'they held it in the village hall and invited the whole "family". Which included *me*.'

Clearly, there is meant to be something self-evidently good about this kind of view of society. Paternalism means roofs over heads and the banishment of rickets and typhoid, thanks to the benevolence of someone who understands that privileges bring their own burdens. On the other hand, it's scarcely bang up-to-date as a social model – unless, in a post-industrial civilisation such as ours which can no longer afford its own social costs, paternalism is due to make a comeback. At the very least, it lacks consistency, to say nothing of efficiency or fairness. And at worst, it's merely an excuse for a kind of social repression with a friendly face.

Something of these thoughts must have been flitting across my face, even though I was doing my best to fill the room with a haze of benign acceptance. I suppose I was looking middle class and a bit doubtful, as if I'd wandered into Giuseppe de Lampedusa's *The Leopard*, and was evidently finding it hard to accommodate this world into mine. So Mr Michael played his ace.

'I know of one estate which is run by a pension fund,' he began, confident that this would tip the balance in my mechanistic, redistributive mind. 'It's just an investment for them – I mean, they've got parts of the West End of London as well. But even there, the chap who has to look after it takes decisions like leaving the underfloor electric heating in a tenant's house, rather than putting in oil-fired, even though the electric costs far more.' He gave me a wise-old-bird look, even though – as ever – he couldn't have been much older than me. 'Behaving like a landowner, in fact.'

He sat back in his (large, leathery) chair and allowed the point to register. What does one say? I wasn't going to pick a fight with him: he was doing me a favour, taking half an hour out of his busy day, giving me details of how the various economic functions of the estate combined (leisure, farming, tenancy, woodland: nothing gross or sensational, unfortunately).

He was also, I would have said, not an especially posh person himself. Somewhere around the level of a country solicitor, I would have put him. Or a vet, maybe. He could almost have been somewhere around my level, except for the patina of grandeur which had rubbed off him from his surroundings, and from his belief in this way of organising things. I couldn't bring myself to hate him at all.

But what, exactly, was his point? That being put in charge of an age-old estate filled with age-old dependants is apt to encourage the same set of mental attitudes in a publicly quoted investment company as it is in someone who's been born and raised to fulfil such a task? That, contrary to what one had been led to believe, a mixture of *noblesse oblige* and latter-day feudalism was such a sempiternal ideal that even the most stingy business would give in to it in the end and go the way of the Lord of the Manor?

Nice work if you can get it, I suppose would be just as true. It obviously struck Mr Michael as incontrovertibly certain, at the same time as it was striking me as being highly ambiguous. I didn't buy the vision. Nor did I buy it when I drove away from his idyll in bright sunshine and with birds singing, only to get hopelessly lost among the roads that criss-crossed the manorial estate, before ending up a hundred yards further down the road on which I'd started, outside the Earl's pub.

So I didn't buy it from Mr Michael, I didn't buy it at Queen Charlotte's Ball and I bought it only grudgingly from Lord Cottesloe: the idea that very socially smart, well-heeled people with titles or connections to titles can justify – can somehow earn – their smartness, wealth, snobbery and the general deference they expect from the rest of society by turning out every now and then to do what's known as their duty. I'm sure the lords lieutenant work hard at being lords lieutenant, and I'm sure Mr Michael's master thinks of himself as a decent man in touch with his ancestral obligations, but there is still a golden thread connecting even these paragons with hysterical Sally and greasy, chiselled, self-absorbed Paul, whose father owned Norway and for whom the connection between having a good time and funding research into the prevention of lung damage in babies must have been as tenuous as a thin mist.

Frankly, I'm not impressed that the Earl of Chutney shows a bit of the eleemosynary temper towards his tenant farmers in the matter of rent-free accommodation, or by throwing a jamboree to celebrate his birthday. He can afford to. He may allow some old boy a low-rent cottage on the estate, but we can assume that the old boy gets a low-rent wage too. And if the Earl of Chutney's books don't balance, he is far more likely, with just enough head-shaking and eye-wiping to make it seem a wrench (quite often for the benefit of a TV crew, these days) to sell out to some pitiless combine which will make them balance. The rate of exchange is heavily weighted in favour of the posh. Doing their duty is the least one could expect of them. Which is why they do it. When Charles Greville stayed with Lord Egremont (the owner of Pet-worth) in 1834, he tearfully described his Lordship's open-air feast for the indigent of the neighbourhood, summing it up with this encomium: 'There was something affecting in the contem-plation of that old man' – Egremont himself – 'rejoicing in the diffusion of happiness and finding keen gratification in relieving the distresses and contributing to the pleasures of the poor.' Affecting only up to a point: at the end of the feast, the poor would have gone back to being poor, while Egremont would have settled in a library armchair and dithered over whether to round off the day with a glass of port or brandy.

You don't even have to be respectable to be upper class and do your duty. Even that greedy degenerate Margaret, Duchess of Argyll – society's blow-fly – acquired a sense of duty in her six-ties and started to save the Argyll Highlanders. She also hunted around for some wretched foundling to bring up. 'The . . . dream I had as a child,' she claimed, 'was to adopt six orphans. From, probably, India or somewhere.' At this level, duty is no more than convenient posture with which to beguile your biographers.

★

The worst offenders by far in this deception are, of course, the royal family. Let us look at some small facts.

Britain's senior royal family members – at the time of writing, the Queen, the Queen Mother, Prince Philip, Prince Charles, Princess Di, Princess Anne, Princes Andrew and Edward and Princess Margaret – live (with the possible exception of Princess Anne and just conceivably of Prince Edward) in conditions of overwhelming luxury, on money provided either by the taxpayer or as the result of royal inheritance (viz. the Duchy of Cornwall for Charles). They are dressed in the finest clothes, eat and drink whatever they please, do no manual work other than what they feel like doing (a bit of light gardening, some tennis), are conveyed all over the world first class. For this, in return, they are prepared to display themselves to the public in a highly selective and controlled fashion and call it their *duty* or even their royal *burden*.

But for the month in which I'm writing, the diary of engagements for the senior royal family members, as issued by the press secretary to the Queen, reads as follows: the Queen has three engagements, Prince Charles has twelve, Princess Diana has *one*, the Duke of Edinburgh has nine, Prince Edward has *one*, Princess Margaret has five, Princess Anne twenty-five and the Queen Mother (God bless her), none at all. Princess Margaret's bookings, it's gratifying to see, tend to be for things like private views at the Queen's Gallery and performances by the Scottish Ballet. Princess Anne's, on the other hand, are for a lot of terrible convocations like the British Knitting and Clothing Export Council and the Commonwealth Magistrates' and Judges' Association: confirmation that she is living up to her image as hardest-working royal with the least prepossessing meet-the-people duties.

Yet, in this context, hard-working is a strictly relative term. Given that the Princess Royal's visits are often compacted into a single day – three trips in twenty-four hours in the

Manchester–Cheshire region, and so on – this still leaves the best part of a fortnight in which she appears to be doing nothing at all. Perhaps she's preparing herself for her next round of engagements. Perhaps she's drafting speeches for the British Knitting and Clothing Export Council. Perhaps she's rushed off her feet. But even if she is, what, pray, is the Princess Margaret (as the diary of engagements affectedly calls her) up to for those long weeks? To say nothing of the Queen. I know the Queen's in her seventies, but three engagements a month would strike me as about the right rate for a nonagenarian, let alone for someone famed for her vitality and robustness.

And yet apologists for the royal family claim obsessively that a) the Queen is a lot cleverer than she appears – really *amazingly* clued up on world affairs and terribly *shrewd*, a great judge of character (although I don't suppose anyone would nowadays care to second John Pearson's fawning slush, *The Ultimate Family*, written ten years ago: 'Elizabeth II can calmly congratulate herself on having presided over the discreet but most effective resurrection of the House of Mountbatten-Windsor'); and b) that she works a lot harder than she actually appears to do, constantly having briefing meetings with the prime minister and her ladies-in-waiting and other court wastrels.

The only gloss I can put on this first point is that I did once see a grovelling TV documentary on the Queen's life: to all intents and purposes she came across as entirely unintellectual, a dimly stolid Sloane, surrounded by an unusual number of hysterical middle-aged and elderly sycophants. As for the second, I can only assume that by not appearing anywhere in public, she's burnishing the monarchy's mystique, Walter Bagehot-style, by making sure that, if no one can actually see her doing nothing, they'll assume she's hard at work doing something somewhere else: justifying the £7 million she drains from the public purse every year.

All so much silage. Somewhere in the post-war settlement, the royal family got it into their heads that they ought to be seen to provide some sort of service, some kind of value for money. It was clearly felt that there ought to be a more open economic relationship between the royal family and the rest of Great Britain, which was putting them up in such unconditional splendour. Thus, the task the royal family decided it had to perform was a loose, ill-specified mish-mash of bringing happiness to the people, providing a sense of continuity in an ever-changing world and giving Britain an identity abroad.

The fact is, though, that this is just a very grand revisiting of that aristocratic guilt which obliges rich, titled landowners to hand out a few freebies to the people for whom they feel responsible. That *noblesse oblige*, that sense of duty which somehow acts as a pay-off for the superb life you've been born to.

It is an indefensible mess, of course. When Fergie, the Duchess of York, was one of the inner circle of royals, what mind-blowing dishonesty, what massive act of self-deception allowed the world to think of her as one of the great and good, merely because she was married to a bloke called Windsor and had opened a couple of hospital wings? What did she think she was doing, posing (as she did) in *Hello!* magazine with a group of bewildered Romanian orphans, acting the part of a titled aid worker? Did she seriously imagine that this would somehow atone for the fact that she'd spent the preceding years squandering £5 million on a repellent new family home, to say nothing of a fortune on a succession of ludicrous frocks and first-class plane tickets?

Even Princess Diana has turned out to be a lemon. At first, everyone forgave her and her berkish husband for being a drain on the state, because she was cute. Now, however, she's aged a bit, and has revealed herself in her true colours: an ageing

Knightsbridge neurotic with two kids, a divorce and a nagging dread that her nose is too big and she's getting wrinkles.

The only good thing in all this is that the tabloids worked out long ago that Di and the rest of the royal family are shockingly over-priced. As a consequence, they've decided to extract some value from the monarchy by tearing it to pieces on a long-term basis. This seems to me to be a entirely reasonable aspect of the economics of being rich and privileged: a kind of redistributive taxation, inflicting misery rather than demanding hard cash. Di, naturally, tries to bargain her way out of this by claiming that she's a latterday saint, but it doesn't work.

Indeed, she reminds me in some ways of the late Lady 'Bubbles' Rothermere. Back in the 1980s, Bubbles was wife to Lord Rothermere, the astoundingly rich owner of the *Daily Mail*. Bubbles owned a vast apartment in Eaton Square, an even larger house in Sussex (it burned down so she had it rebuilt in replica), a place on Fifth Avenue, a place in Mustique and yet another place in Beverly Hills. She was driven around in a Bentley by her chauffeur. She was indecently fat and she drank like W.C. Fields. She had in fact become a kind of metropolitan joke, a Lady Docker of her times, a byword for self-indulgence, copiously pilloried in *Private Eye*.

In retrospect, it's hard to know how self-aware she really was and how much merely the taffeta-brained aristo. In interviews she used to come out with remarks like this – for the *Tatler*, in this instance: 'There is, of course, my love for all my friends and my great appreciation of people and life itself. And my notoriety,' she went on, 'is not just by the way. It's not accidental. As I told you, I am first and foremost an actress.'

While granting this audience, late at night at Annabel's club, she apparently laid into three bowls of onion soup with croutons and a quart of champagne on the rocks before swaying off to catch the last Concorde of the day. This was more or less typical.

But here's a funny thing. I used to teach Bubbles' younger daughter 'O' level English. This is perfectly true. It was at the time that I was hacking about London, cramming the public-school drop-outs for their As. One day, this funny little bloke with an office off Kensington High Street called me in.

'Eaton Square,' he said, scratching his thighs. 'Can you get over there on your bike?'

So I did, and tied my old grid to the railings outside Bubbles' fabulous apartment, beneath the disapproving scowls of the resident dowagers and Kuwaitis. I then met the daughter and eventually met Bubbles herself. And she was indeed a Hogarthian caricature. The apartment's priceless furnishings and ankle-deep carpets were littered with dust, threatening letters from British Airways' legal department (non-payment of Concorde tickets, as a rule) and the odd mound of dogshit where the tremulously bowelled shih-tzu had been startled by one of Bubbles' party guests. Stepping into her flat was like stepping into *Shortly After The Marriage*.

And when Bubbles herself emerged wigless from her powdery boudoir at midday to say hello to her daughter and gaze uncertainly at me, she would be wrapped in a tent-sized nightie covered in make-up and food spillages. Shortly after that, she would retreat again to her bed, followed by a knowing serf with a tray containing a full English fry-up (sausages, bacon, black pudding) and a bottle of Moët & Chandon. Later in the day (I knew this because I taught sometimes in the morning, sometimes at lunchtime, sometimes in the evening, according to Bubbles' caprice), she could be seen sweeping down the corridors of the apartment, dressed in gigantic watered-silk dresses and shouting for Bloody Marys.

From my position in the domestic hierarchy (well below that of the gardener, marginally above the shih-tzu) I was able to observe her take her multitudes of phone calls, berate her hatchet-faced social secretary, bellow for her Bentley, yell for drinks, wail greetings at her friends and generally devote herself to what appeared to be little more than a procession of self-gratification, mindless hob-nobbing and childish profligacy, lived in conditions of the most extreme material comfort.

And yet what she was proudest of, what she wanted outsiders to remark upon, what she drew attention to in her interviews, were her charity work and her awards ('Putting people together from wide walks of life and just being international,' as she once characterised her services to the nation). These prizes were promiscuously strewn around her drawing room: over here, a thing awarded to Women of Our Time; over there, a charitable fund-raising certificate; and over one of the fireplaces, a Woman of the Year Award from some risible institute in the States. They stood around like church tracts among the empty champagne glasses, vases of costly flowers and cigarette ends. They looked ridiculous, unbelievable. Surely Bubbles could not have expected us to believe that beneath that bloated exterior, there was a woman with depth, a woman who cared?

But this, I now see, is typical. An extreme case, maybe: the physical evidence of Bubbles contradicted her wishful thinking so completely, it was like Lytton Strachey putting school boxing cups on his mantelpiece. But these palliatives, these efforts to justify one's existence: they're the same whether they're charitable awards for Bubbles Rothermere, or whether they're a grandee's notions of duty. It's a fraud – a fraud some people take more seriously than others, but a fraud all the same.

And who is the most conspicuous of these fraudsters? Who is the Lite version of Bubbles Rothermere? None other than the Princess of Wales. All that cant she came out with in the *Panorama* interview about wanting to be the queen of people's hearts ... as if this would actually distract our attention from the truth of the Princess of Wales: which is that she's good at having tennis lessons, getting her hair done, shopping, eating in restaurants and turning up now and then at launch parties in preposterously expensive dresses.

If I had to characterise this state of affairs, I would call it *infantilising*. The whole idea of being of high estate contains elements of being wiser and cleverer, to say nothing of richer and more powerful. Those who are grander than us, those who are part of, or just related to, the landowners and officer classes, presume to know better than us. They're older, somehow; more mature. We, the rest of society, should simply get on with our less finished, less grown-up lives while the grandees do those things which only grandees can truly know about.

This is one reason why the Queen is the archetypal matriarch, the mother of the nation. Why else should monarchists get so emotional about an evidently none-too-bright grandma with a big pile in the home counties? Love of the Queen doesn't make sense, but, as Bagehot was keen to point out ('The mystic reverence, the religious allegiance, which are essential to a true monarchy, are imaginative sentiments that no legislature can manufacture in any people'), it isn't meant to. Monarchists love the Queen because she's the essential wise mother. Which is why it's always been impossible to imagine her fucking Prince Philip: it's like trying to imagine your parents at it. And it's why politicians can never bring themselves to talk publicly about getting rid of her. The whole thing would stink of matricide.

And what goes for her goes, in diminishing degrees, for the rest of them. So the archetypal lord, the Jungian peer of the realm, is a luminous old patriarch of some sort. That's how I always imagine lords to be, anyway, and I'm always obscurely disappointed when one of them turns out to be in his thirties, or

131

worse, still at Eton. Ladies are little queens, silver-haired Lady Bountifuls, like the nineteenth-century Marchioness of London-derry, eternally dishing out tea and fruit cake to their children, the spavined tenant farmers and general serfs who owe their existence to the higher orders. Baronets, of course, being *parvenus* invented by James I, are more like sleazy older brothers or Alan Rickman. I actually met a baronet once, and to be honest, he was only marginally sleazy – more like a very well-bred, disarmingly friendly housemaster, even though he was only three years older than me. (I did watch him knock over a glass of wine, though, which gave me a vicious little thrill, seeing his essential, humdrum frailty exposed.)

And so, the way grown-ups tend to, posh people like to con us with the idea that it's not all fun being grown-up, even though that's how it looks: the burden of duty validates the whole upper–lower, senior–junior relationship. 'I'm not doing this because I like it, I'm doing this because I have to. Think yourself lucky you don't.'

All this gave a new emphasis, therefore, to my charity gift fairs. What with it becoming increasingly wintry, people were now starting to barricade themselves in well-heated semi-private places. Charity gift fairs (like their purely mercantile cousins, house-party sales) are a big thing in the months before Christmas: 'Lovers of traditional baby clothes,' Lady Celestria told me, 'are always well served at fairs, as are men who like embroidered linen handkerchiefs.' And your charity gift fair not only gives you some-where pleasant to go on a cold night, it also enables you to do your *duty*, in an urban, acquisitive manner. I sampled a few, but with one exception, they collapsed into a blur of Ascot men without the tail-coats and yet more willowy wives; the difference between the gift fairs and Royal Ascot being that – at the fairs –

the women radiated the kind of ferocious intensity that only Sloane women can when surrounded by garbage that they desperately want to acquire for themselves.

I can't bring myself to describe a charity gift fair I went to in Kensington (an acre of Sloanes with a monobrowed boy in the middle trying to sell illuminated bow ties, and wringing his own neck as he tried to flog a tie to a dismissive, pearl-heavy middle-aged woman – 'It's musical as well!'). Nor another in the chic Hurlingham Club in Fulham. Instead I'll recall the champagne reception for HRH the Crown Princess Katherine of Yugoslavia I got myself invited to.

This was a fund-raising drive for a charity which brought aid and assistance to the people of what used to be Yugoslavia, and it was held in a fabulously high-tone leather goods shop in Bond Street, W1. The shop was filled with about a hundred drawling suits and braying women in tiny black frocks. The charity raffle, unlike your more conventional suburban sort (home-made sponge cakes, self-assembly paper racks) offered such prizes as champagne from Moët, perfume from Guerlain and the chance for two people to stay at a five-star hotel in Cannes. And of course, there were the exquisite leather bags themselves, ranged on shelves all around the guests.

And when the Crown Princess got to her feet to deliver a litany about death, brutality and disease, she was interrupted by a chorus of voices shouting at each other: 'Hello, *darling*!' followed by, 'No, not you! It's your lovely wife I want!' A balding smoothie leaned over to his friend and said, quite loudly, 'I spent two minutes at Tony's party before coming over here, and this is a *much* bigger affair.'

Martin Bell, the BBC's nerveless reporter from the Yugoslavian war front, was standing at one end of the shop, dressed in a brown jacket and a pair of Hush Puppies. I admiringly pointed out this icon of the liberal, humane world to a raven-haired woman in statutory short black dress, and she said, 'Well, I spoke to Martin Bell, and he was so *disappointing!*'

I said that he'd been to Yugoslavia, you know.

'Oh, fat and everything,' she answered. 'I suppose he doesn't want to talk about his work,' she went on. 'He'd have been more interested in mine, probably.'

At this moment, a blonde woman with Brussels sprout-sized pearl earrings marched up. 'You,' said the blonde woman, pointing at the raven-haired one, 'were in the dodgem with Jamie Hewitt!'

'Yes, *I was!*' screamed the raven-haired one. 'It was such fun, but it was in *all* the papers the next day. It was *so* embarrassing!'

Hewitt, you will recall, was the man with whom the Princess of Wales publicly confessed to having had an affair, in her *Panorama* interview. This was the man who had fucked the future (as she then was) Queen of England. And as it turned out, he'd also fucked the raven-haired woman in front of me. She'd been all over the *Daily Mail*, pictured in her dodgem with Hewitt who, at the time, looked, it must be said, like a man in front of a fruit machine which won't stop paying out.

I was so stunned by this sudden intelligence that it took me a while to realise that the woman had vanished into the mob before I could frame any really prurient questions. I then glimpsed her on the far side of the room, leaning against some exquisitely turned leatherware, but a man with a large grin on his face interposed himself between us.

'You should buy *lots* of raffle tickets,' he said to the blonde woman with the Brussels sprout earrings. 'I've made £600 already!'

I stared at him, unable to register even the feeblest protest. Didn't he know that there was a war on? By the time he had gone, chortling to himself, the raven-haired woman was nowhere to be seen. The blonde gave me a watermelon smile. 'I've got a photographic memory,' she said. 'I only have to make a car journey once and I can remember it *exactly*, provided I'm on the same side, driver's or passenger's, that is. I think it must be wonderful to have a vocation.'

She flashed her teeth at me again. Abruptly, I found I couldn't stand it any more. So much pointless talk, so much extravagance, so much show in the service of duty. Like Queen Charlotte's Ball, like the Marchioness of Londonderry, like subsidised chicken stuffing, like Bubbles Rothermere: *ex post facto* palliatives and tendentious guilt money. I left and wandered out into the sparkling Bond Street night, before catching the Tube home in a denunciatory fog.

SEVEN

Shortly after that, however, things looked up. By a mixture of guile and good luck, I got myself invited to a Sloane's birthday party in Kensington. It was being thrown by Charlotte, the *Debrett's* woman who'd told me about life at Sherborne School for Girls. I was almost weepily grateful to wangle the invitation, as it got me out of the run of we-take-anyone season events to which I had condemned myself, and into something a little more select; a little more personal. I was also gratified because I had been avidly – addictedly, even – reading the glossies (*Harpers & Queen, Country Life, Tatler* now littered my floor) and at once began to persuade myself that the event was bound to appear in 'Jennifer's Diary'.

A confession: by this time, I'd developed something of a compulsion for reading high-priced tat. Why? Because, whatever else the high-society glossies do, they make a very good job of selling posh people to the rest of the world. *Tatler* (circulation, 85,370) and *Harpers* (circulation, 85,450)) are like *The National Geographical:* bulletins from another world, consumed and pored over by aliens like me in the privacy of our suburban front rooms.

Not that the whole operation is a fan-club. While I was serving my time with the smart end of the Yellow Press, *Tatler/Harpers* were running all sorts of prurient stuff about the upper classes. Over here, Airlie Castle ('Gloomy vibes hang over the ruined keep') has been looted of Lord Airlie's furniture and fittings, apparently by a couple of plausible Americans. Over there, Lord and Lady Brocket are messily divorcing, while Lord Brocket (already famous for making jokes about Hiroshima to Japanese business associates, and doing a Golders Green Yiddisher accent at a barmitzvah), has been banged up for a £4.5 million insurance scam involving the organised theft of part of his priceless collection of Ferraris. Earl Spencer, brother of Diana, Princess of Wales, has not only gone on record as calling his wife 'thick' but has now apparently run off with a South African woman. (He is also, let us not forget, forever yoked in the public's mind with Old Etonian ex-jailbird Darius Guppy, who was best man at his wedding and is now even more famous as yet another upper-class chancer whose insurance scam – involving gems rather than Ferraris – got him sent down for five years in 1993). And now Countess Waldegrave ('racy, raven-haired, chain-smoking beauty') has started telling the papers of her 'years of fear' with the Earl ...

But this only forms a small part of the whole. And if you spend your time trawling through four hundred pages a month of remorseless high society, then it becomes clear that the bulk of *Harpers* and *Tatler* is quality advertising for the idle upper classes, done with all the queasy aplomb you might expect. In other words, for every tale of insanity, sexual turpitide and moral depravity, you get about five depositions of unimpeachable good character, artistic and business flair and personal beauty.

'The Duchess of Marlborough,' for example, according to *Tatler*, 'is not only chatelaine, wife and mother, but also a fine artist.' And there, indeed, she is, blonde and blindingly dentate, talking about 'art and inspiration' in a succession of impossibly grand settings. She is also wearing a pair of trousers that cost £2,800. Lantern-jawed India Hicks ('gorgeous granddaughter of Earl Mountbatten of Burma . . . trained as a photographer in Paris before Ralph Lauren snapped her up') turns up in *Harpers* one month, modelling 'a light, soft summer wardrobe of linens and silks' and in *Tatler* the next, as one of the '200 great dates of the decade'. A *Harpers* hack 'intercepts the Air Squadron, the most dashing flying club in the world', and finds it, unsurprisingly, laden with grandees such as the Marquess of Milford Haven and Sir Adrian Swire. The Marquess of Bath, in a blatant piece of *Tatler* promotion, turns out to be a great bloke ('a true eccentric in the way only the truly classy can afford to be'), despite his wifelets and his murals of penises and foetuses.

Does it matter? Does anyone care? Or is it just swank wall-paper? If you're in my position it matters, because these people, via these publications, are setting an impossibly high standard. It's bad enough having to trawl, anonymous and unbidden, around the smart set, without having these paragons dangled before your eyes. How can one possibly look like these people, let alone live like them? How can anyone be so glossy, so measurably perfect?

And this is just at the flash end of things, the end most obvi-ously designed for public consumption. At the other, tweedier, end of publishing, you have your *Country Life*, your *Field*, your *Horse and Hound*. These sell the posh life just as assiduously as the glamour publications. But they do it in such a discreet, indirect way that the process is almost more seductive. It's like being taken by the elbow by some titled fart in a decent bit of thornproof, led through the Old Hall (reeking of beeswax, carpeting and good

English flowers) and being inducted into the real world of posh country people: a world of fresh breezes, dependable red faces, decency, reticence, good humour, fish, sensible footwear, headscarves, dogs, love of the land, roaring fires, outhouses, knowing what to do with dead edible animals – an English Arcadia, in other words, the modern inheritance of the world of Gainsborough, Stubbs and Reynolds.

Thus, a typical issue of the *Field* kicks off with an endearingly and (I presume) unintentionally humorous cover shoutline – 'Boom Year for Grouse?' – before plunging into the Irish Red Setter ('a rough-shooter's dream'), In Line for the Covey, A Close Escape for Dartmoor's Wild Ponies, and so on. This is practical, level-headed countryman's arcanum, the kind of stuff of which I was wholly unaware until I bought a copy of the *Field*. My experience of the countryside is normally so short term, so urban in its terms of reference, so brutally exploitative (just give me the scenery and fuck off) that just flicking through the magazine makes me feel decent.

This is less true of *Horse and Hound*, given the way *H&H* comes across as a kind of *Hello!* for nags and their titled owners. But it too carries the authentic, businesslike tang of proper outdoor pursuits. 'Going off to boarding school?' demands an advert. 'Can you take your horse/pony with you at no cost for livery?' *Shooting Times*, I must confess, left me a bit uneasy ('Superb day for talented young guns') with its ads for British-made Live Catch Traps and various gunsafes – but then, what else did I expect in a magazine with the word *shooting* in the title?

Country Life, however, is odder than either of these. Sometimes it grips the nettle of change pretty damn firmly (interviews with Tony Blair and Chris Smith; Lord Wyatt's daughter models yet more Ralph Lauren). Sometimes it's starkly reactionary (that blow-by-blow listing of the lords lieutenant of England; an interview with the Duke of Westminster). For much of the time, though, it wanders in a loopily stuffy manner among the artifacts and obsessions of well-heeled trad English life: cheese-making, silverware, gardening, general foodstufs ('Sausage supply secured'), plasterwork, embroidery. And in whatever's left over – usually about half the magazine – it devotes itself to (literally) selling the Grand Life as hard as it can. It is so successful at this, that despite having a fairly modest circulation of 51,500, it is known as something of a cash-cow for its owners, IPC, so much money does it pull in from the advertisers. Thus, it is awash with ads for eye-wateringly fabulous houses and estates, paintings, antiques, regimental ties and unburstable trousers. In this respect, it's no more than a weekly sales catalogue with some emollient prose thrown in. And yet you can't mistake its true class affinities, its blinding sincerity.

The result is morbidly engrossing. You end up wading, breathless with disbelief, first of all through a swamp of ads for castles, manor houses, thousand-acre Grade II listed properties, million-pound palaces, buildings that are so rare and costly that the rapacious estate agents won't even name a price. Then the properties come to a close and you find yourself staring haggardly at a society photo-portrait of some splendid young woman who keeps horses, wears almost no make-up (thus emphasising the flawlessness of her English skin, soft and pink as uncooked chicken) and who is about as socially comprehensible to someone like me as an Inuit. And then it's on through a gallimaufry of furniture sales, silverware restoration, fox-hunting and grandee profiles, before grinding to a halt in a welter of regular columns ('In My Garden') and small ads ('Have your ancestors or coat of arms researched economically'). It's a trip through the mind of some great, imaginary buffer: a stumble through the attic of a class's sensibility.

But is it seductive? Well, in a crumbling, smelly sort of way, I suppose it is. And this is because I share – by definition, I guess – that suburban, middle-class hankering after those things which suburbia pastiches and reduces for the common man.

So when I see a staggering Grade II job with sweeping lawns and outhouses and gravel drives, I look, in a very real sense, on the Platonic ideal of the house I'm actually living in. Like anyone who's ever voluntarily entered a National Trust property, I con all that creaky old furniture and those gravy-glazed paintings and those big rooms with high, mullioned windows, and I drift into a middle-class, National Trust reverie. I see myself as the generous, humorous, decent, fair, non-flatulent, quietly knowledgeable, rich and probably titled owner of such things. I see myself being deferred to by the local peasants and worshipped by the cringeing, bourgeois professionals of the nearest town (Reigate or Newbury, say). I even see myself sporting those frightful clothes in a relaxed and congenial manner.

It is, of course, a precarious little fantasy, because even if I had all the money it takes to own and run one of these piles, I couldn't live out of London anyway (countryside is just interminable, like a novel with no plot). And *Country Life* itself, with its agglomeration of farts, freezing properties, equine girls, bullying furniture and thuggish country pursuits, reminds me of precisely what is wrong with country life, at the same time as it dresses it up in a great catalogue of bourgeois aspirations. It is a retrograde life, a life whose boundaries are clearly set in the mid-1950s with a touch of early Edwardian thrown in. It is a life which oughtn't to be lived. But it still beguiles, when I've had an off day, or when I'm just feeling stuffy and uncommunicative.

All this, however, is just a part of a sinister pathology which gradually revealed itself most acutely in the society pages of *Harpers* and *Tatler*. You see, I knew perfectly well that constantly exposing myself to the glossies' smug, envy-provoking nonsense would have an effect. If you force yourself to look at pictures of rich, smart folk having a good time and (in the society diaries) being pissed and full of themselves in some very nice places, you will start to wish you were one of those people. If you lurk on the outermost fringes of their world, you might also develop a sense that somewhere nearer the centre, people are having a better, more self-indulgent, more arrogant time than you are, and begin to wonder how on earth you can get a piece of this rich alcoholic stuff for yourself. But I didn't realise how bad things were until I became aware that I was taking the society pages seriously.

This was not good. For years, like any normal person, I'd treated 'Jennifer's Diary' and 'Bystander' with the kind of hostile derision they deserve. I mean, what possible justification is there, in this day and age, for *so* many pictures of posh, rich people simply pleasuring themselves? Where is the sense in this parade of giggling socialites? I can understand wanting to see a photo of Elton John in the back of a limo, or Demi Moore, or anyone you might have heard of and therefore feel a sense of possession towards; the weird possessiveness the public tends to feel about any big celeb.

But why on earth should I want to see a picture of the Earl of Pembroke dressed in a kind of DIY cavalier's uniform? What is the significance of Lady Victoria Scott in a hat shaped like a ship's capstan? What's the point of Lord Dalmeny in a kilt? Does Miss Isabella Anstruther-Gough-Calthorpe in a cardigan at Lady Mary Gaye Curson's party at Claridge's have anything to do with anything? Yes, we need these people as icons of hatred and envy; yes we need to be titillated and appalled by their goings-on. But do we need such a super-abundance of photographic accounts every month?

Try telling me that. In the space of a few weeks I had gone

from the decent and rational view I'd held for years – that the society pages were both hilarious and despicable – to a condition of guilty, painful relish. My eyes would glaze over with yearning as I drank in the details of a Mayfair piss-up full of people I'd never heard of. Over here, I would light upon a dog-faced girl in a décolleté evening gown, a flute of champagne clutched in her fat hand. Over there, I would sigh with envy at some dotard, red-faced with drink and exertion, squiring his tart around the premises. And over there, I would simper along with the pretty children of a lord and think to myself how sweet they were and how lucky to be born into a world of such beauty, quality and privilege. I would end up, after a bad session with 'Jennifer's Diary', fanning myself and whimpering gently, like one of those pathetic deluded old women who appear on TV every now and then saying how lovely the Queen is.

In other words, I started to lose my reason. Instead of taking things rationally, acknowledging the central fact of my existence – that I'm suburban, middle class, immutably so – I started to want to *be* one of these smug fuckers. I wanted to taste that champagne, sniff that scent, suck on a bolster-shaped cigar. I wanted to creep into the corners of those postage-stamp-sized accounts of another world and fondle the damask tablecloths and manorial wood-work. I wanted to be like the posh girls and boys (grinning fiercely, displaying clean, well-toned flesh); or, failing that, like the oldsters – trimmed, tucked and tanned. I knew that the pro-paganda element was as hard at work on the diary pages as any-where in the magazine (compare today's compliant 'Bystander' with the crueller, more sardonic version edited by the late Mark Boxer in the 1980s), but I still fell for it.

And this is why I was so worked up at the prospect of attend-ing the Sloane's birthday party. In the great scheme of things – in the 'Jennifer's Diary' scheme of things – I knew in my heart that it was an event not even worth mentioning. But from my grimy perspective, it was a taste of that fatuously enthralling world from which I'd been excluded for so long.

It was going to be black tie, a hundred and thirty guests and a suite of rooms in Kensington. What's more, Charlotte – unmarried, working in the antiques business – was not only *Debrett's*, not only Sherborne School for Girls, but a proper London Trustafarian. She had a pile of money sitting in trust for her in a private bank and had just used some of the capital to buy herself a nice little house in Chelsea. And she liked things from The General Trading Company in Sloane Street. So how did I get invited?

Well, Sloanes can be quite friendly people until they get to know you. They like to have a rich social life, and this by definition entails dragging in strangers from outside the run of things and giving them a chance to perform. Once I'd managed to blag an introduction to one Sloane, they'd quite often introduce me to a friend, who might pass me on to a third. As you go further up the scale, other-class strangers like me increasingly acquire the characteristics of court jesters, who must entertain for their privileges. Ultimately, you get the Queen, who can be as dull as cardboard while at the same time expecting those more interesting and talented than her to make up the cultural shortfall. Sloanes are like that, except that, since they have less to offer materially than the Queen, they are slightly less demanding of their try-out friends.

Only slightly less demanding, mind you. I didn't really know this Charlotte woman; nor she me. I was there on appro, as it were. Being a writer, I was obviously expected to bring some of that Brendan Behan lyrical craziness, some of that Wildean brilliance to the party. At that time, Charlotte hadn't realised what an uninspiring fellow I really am, so there was everything to gain, from her point of view.

Sensing that more was going to be asked of me than is the case at the average stand-up-and-shout, I did some research. This entailed boning up on the two classiest fiction writers I could find on my bookshelves: Anthony Powell (Eton and Oxford, friend of Waugh's, solid bet) and Henry Green (Eton and Oxford, friend of Waugh's, likewise). It didn't work. Their protagonists (from *A Buyer's Market* and *Living*) seemed to spend the whole time making a bollocks of things ('It was evident that the subject of Stringham could supply no basis for discussion between us' . . . 'Then he was rude to her,' etc.) – the main difference between me and them being that they habitually did it in the most *soigné* surroundings. Irrelevant, I thought, starting to sink into a light depression. I turned to the first etiquette book I could find, to see if that had any bright ideas. This turned out to be *The Good Housekeeping Everyday Etiquette* primer. I read, 'Some people seem to have no trouble at all in keeping a conversation going . . . others, whether shy, self-conscious or just inexperienced, find the whole business of talking to people they hardly know thoroughly alarming.'

I nodded morosely at this. The remedy?

'When you know that an event where you'll be talking to people is coming up, try and find out something about the other guests in advance. This will give you useful clues as to the things they might like to talk about.'

With a cry of rage I hurled the book across the room. Was I seriously supposed to ring up this *Debrett's* Sloane whose party it was and quiz her for half an hour on who was likely to be at my table? Ask about their children, their bisexuality, their verrucas, their favourite brands of balsamic vinegar?

To take my mind off things, I spent a long time choosing a present which I hoped would acknowledge the social distance between us while at the same time suggesting that we had too much in common to keep us on opposite sides of the canyon which divides bourgeois from smart. I got her, at enormous expense, a book of photos by Cartier-Bresson (arty, I thought, but non-committally so), which, so far as I know, she hasn't yet got round to opening. A friend of hers took the present off me as I arrived and deposited it on top of a cone of gifts by the front entrance, so I don't know that she's even held the book in her hands. Perhaps she's too busy. Perhaps she gets other people to enjoy her presents for her.

As I handed the gift over, I sensed that my DJ trousers were about to fall down again, and that my self-tied tie was beginning to look a trifle anarchic. My homework came back to haunt me. I could see myself as a cruel caricature in someone else's novel: the hopeless, aspiring, middle-class buffoon, whom everyone despises and who ends up dead or discovered in a cupboard, wearing women's clothing.

Even so, as I stumbled up the steps to the reception room, it crossed my mind that at least no one had actually stopped me and flung me back down the steps. I was there, at least. I'd been sent a stiff white card invitation, I'd put on my DJ, got the wife out in her evening dress, handed the invitation over at the entrance and I was *in*.

The principal reception room was tall and thin and lit by coloured lights so you couldn't properly see what was going on. There were pots of gnarled dead sticks arranged around the walls, following the fashion of the day, which ordained that gnarled dead sticks were the smart anti-greenery to have. It was very hot and there were a lot of people (none of whom I knew, of course) shouting at each other in the red and green gloom. At first glance, they looked like a crowd of shoppers from Beauchamp Place, stuck in a very big lift. There were several Harvey Nicks women –

wild-eyed, stick-thin, sucking on their appetite-suppressant cigs and jawing at each other. They held their heads back and jutted their chins forward, collapsing from time to time into screams of laughter. There was also a mixture of sullen, jowly, thirtyish men and rather younger bucks, making conversation with the women, or, more desperately, with each other.

The first words I could make out came from a bulging Nicholas Soames lookalike, who said, 'Course, the trouble with Kenya is it's a bloody lovely country, but the people are bloody impossible.'

I stood around feeling like a leper and wondering how soon I could decently leave. My wife, fortunately, is better at handling these situations than I am. She toughed our way into a conversation with a tall man with thinning, greased-back hair and a fierce Japanese woman, who, it transpired, was big in the Conservative Party. Already drunk on one glass of champagne, I heard myself shouting at the Japanese woman that all Japanese food was a con trick, and how could anyone be expected to live on a teaspoonful of raw fish and thimble of rice when they're six feet tall? Then I was distracted by a couple of Sloane girls next to me.

One was tall, blonde and wearing a gilded lamé dress. The other was short, large-bosomed and crammed into some black trousers. They both had the voice. And they were both attacking a boy in white tie and tails.

'We know you!' they shrieked at the boy. 'We know you! Where do we know you from? We *know* we know you! Come on!' They started plucking at his shirt front and punching him in the ribs. It was a thrilling moment for me: because in the half-dark, at the correct angle, the frolicsome trio could *almost* have appeared in one of those postage-stamp photos in 'Bystander' or 'Jennifer's Diary'. In that instant they looked truly authentic: well-heeled, young, posh, glossy, stupid, *Tatler* material. I lapsed into a reverie. Observing my dreamy expression as I stared at the girls, the tall bloke with the thinning hair said, 'They hunt in a pack, you know.'

'Cor,' I said.

A full sit-down dinner for a 130 then followed, in a dining room which gave directly off the reception room.

I was bunged on a table in the middle. The dining room had some more expressionist lighting effects and more gnarled sticks, and was lined all the way round with blood-red velvet curtains. There was the statutory boy, girl disposition of the guests around our table, ten of us, staring apprehensively at each other and at the immense pile of flowers in the centre. It felt a little like Queen Charlotte's Ball, but more leeringly intimate. From behind me, I heard some fellow explode with satisfaction. 'Excellent bottle of champagne!' he shouted. '*Excellent* bottle!'

My heart leaped a little. A night of debauch? As François de la Rochefoucauld wrote in 1784, after a visit to the Duke of Grafton, 'I have heard things mentioned in good society which would be in the grossest taste in France. The sideboard too is furnished with a number of chamber pots and it is a common practice to relieve oneself whilst the rest are drinking.' Would it be the same here? People pissing in public, like real gents? Were we to be like Fielding's Squire Western, who went to bed 'so drunk that he could not see'? Was this to be an orgy of groaning and braying, of top-drawer obscenities? Berkoff's *Decadence*?

I thought I could make out, on the far side of the table, a middle-aged woman saying, 'I've got the most *marvellous* gynaecologist . . . my tubes were in such a *state* . . . had to stand on my head . . .'

I tried talking houses with the woman on my right. ('She's *terribly* grand,' my hostess confided off-puttingly later on. 'Comes from a huge pile.') This woman wore an expensive-looking evening dress, had a fungal complexion and teeth like menhirs. She began to tell me the story of how she and her husband (a middle-aged, stony-faced man on the far side) had found a rat in the Aga. Well, OK, I decided, as she gabbled on about doing a joint of pork and finding this toasted furry object at the back of the oven, perhaps that's what the golden creatures in the society pages talk about as the cameras flash. Perhaps they discuss their gynaecologists and the dead creatures inside their cookers: another confirmation of the power of the solitary, silent, image to imbue the banal with significance. So I struggled along with my usual collection of eyebrow-wagglings and noises of hilarious disbelief.

And then I had a whiff of the real thing. I found myself suddenly and vertiginously in a conversation with Mrs Teeth about a *mutual acquaintance*: just like two characters out of *A Dance to the Music of Time*; just like two posh people really having a conversation with each other about someone they both know, instead of one posh person politely suffering the monologue of another person who must have seemed entirely unqualified for the place he currently occupied.

It was Harry, the Scottish dancing instructor. Of course, I didn't exactly *know* Harry, I'd merely *met* him. But this was a distinction to which Mrs Teeth was too polite to allude and which I wasn't prepared to make explicit. So I went along with the fiction that I knew Harry, the Old Etonian Scottish dancing instructor, knew him like *that*, and just let her unravel verbally before me: 'Well, of course, I met him when my parents decided to throw a dance for me, *the way one's parents did.*'

This was my cue to laugh sympathetically and chuck in plenty of noddings and twinkles around the eyes, as if having your parents throw a dance for you was precisely the cross I'd had to bear as a teenager.

'He's a Gloucestershire boy, like I was a Gloucestershire girl. He was at Eton.'

Yes, of course he was. As, indeed, I might have been, in the half-light, with the din of guests all around me. My voice cracked slightly as I did my best to converge with her voice. And of course, he could dance, couldn't he! Old Harry! What a dancer and Old Etonian! Great chap, I urged, trying desperately to sound *up*.

'So I knew a few girls, of course, the way one did, but I didn't know any *boys* at all! Except Harry. He was charming, I seem to remember.'

I wondered whether or not to observe that the place where I'd met him had been full of shamingly hot, sweaty Sloanes and that I couldn't honestly grasp the point of Scottish dancing. This wouldn't have done, of course. So I lied. I took a deep breath and claimed that the whole of my encounter with him had been ter-rific fun, kilts, red wine, stamping, bruising and dislocations, eight-some reels, hell of a good time. I did my best to pitch my voice somewhere around the level of a hyper-animated Ascot drawl, coming from somewhere further back in the throat than my normal squawk and overlaid with a cover of nasal *hur, hurs*. I thought I was managing it fairly convincingly. It felt like a con-versation – awkward, artificial, bolted together, a Frankenstein conversation, admittedly, but nevertheless, a conversation on equal terms between me and a posh person. And then I realised that she was gazing abstractedly over my shoulder. Then she realised that I'd realised, and jerked her face back towards mine.

'Sorry!' she said brightly. 'I'm just looking over your shoulder to see what everyone's wearing.'

There was no malice in her voice. Just the frank acknowledge-ment that from time to time, one was going to dial out of the intercourse and do something more interesting.

I wondered what to do next. At that moment I overheard her husband fruitily patronising my wife. 'And what sort of car do you drive?' he said. 'A nice little Fiat, I suppose? Something like that?' Mrs Teeth must have picked this up too, because while I toyed with my main course and debated with myself whether or not to feel betrayed, she started on about her own car, and how she'd tried a Discovery but found it too wide for the London streets and had ended up buying a Volvo. Hardly less wide, one would have thought, but apparently there is a difference. 'Well, yes, of course it's an estate, ha, ha, but that's because you have to have room for six children, don't you?'

Once again, I felt uneasy. Nothing really seemed to have changed since hysterical Sally. Conversations between smart people simply did not go this way. They were surely less tentative, less jolting, more obviously driven by a common sense of what the dynamics of a conversation were. Those paragons from *Tatler*, I had to believe, were having long, seamless, laughter-filled exchanges full of names and places and past events and any other shared material. I could hear it in my head: Tamsin – Jeremy – St Kitt's – broken-down old MG – three bottles of poo – No! – Ran a wine bar for Alex – total druggie now, Mummy says – allowance – he saw you – Antonia – Thursday – couldn't believe it! – Really really big house in Kent – Georgina! – Telling Caroline he was joining Daddy for shooting – new GTi – such a bastard, oh, complete bastard – have one of mine. That kind of thing.

For a long moment I sat there, next to my dinner companion, feeling as if we were two ruined buildings facing each other across an empty street, each vacantly inspecting the other for signs of life.

In fact, it felt the way it feels if I ever venture down Sloane Street, or into one of the swank shops around Brompton Cross. It's not as if I'm not entitled to be there, but there's no question that I don't fit in. Among the smart shops of SW1 and SW3 I feel perpetually obliged to account for my presence in some way. Fingering the Armani suits or gawping at the contents of one of Joseph's shops, it's clear that with my chainstore duds, my air of belligerent unease and my dismal haircut, I don't belong there, any more than I belong in the streets of Addis Ababa. I long to tell the shop proprietors, and indeed, the passers-by, that although I may look a bit common, I wash daily and have all my own teeth, and that I'll be gone soon.

I did once try to butch it out at Harvey Nichols' top-floor cafeteria by standing at the coffee bar and slowly and deliberately finishing an espresso in full view of the skeletal women and permed men who haunt the place. But it was hard. The coffee was extremely hot, I was wearing my overcoat indoors in order to conceal the food stains on my pullover and I was sweating like a wrestler. It was also clear that, unlike the ultra-sociable Sloanes, I was on my own, with no prospect of things changing.

The same would be true, of course, if I stood gloomily in some hard-man pub in, say, South Shields. But it comes back to the relative narrowness of the social difference between me and the Sloanes and the chasm between me and the hard men of South Shields. I ought to feel almost comfortable in a place like Harvey Nichols, whereas I'd expect to feel deeply uncomfortable in a pub in South Shields. As it transpires, when I *was* in a pub in South Shields, I felt merely morbid rather than threatened. I'm close to the Sloane world, so close I can blag my way into its birthday parties without looking too much like an object of pity or a token black, but I just can't break through the millimetre of social distinction which separates us.

Staring at Mrs Teeth, I wondered whether or not to broach the subject with her. She might have wanted to talk about it. Except that she was off again, filling the agonising pause (for which I was largely responsible) with stuff about how she always found herself reading books about how you get your children to read books, or how to cook a dinner for a hundred people.

Fortunately, it was now sparkler time. Picture the scene: a room, filled with a 130 guests in evening dress, the walls a sea of blood-coloured velvet, candlelight gleaming from the tables; the low, continuous roar of well-bred voices like waves on a shingle beach. There are young faces, disintegrating oldsters, wracked-looking middle-aged parents with dark circles under their eyes. There is a sense of wealth and privilege in the air. Then we light our sparklers, and sing 'Happy Birthday' to Charlotte. 'It's all right,' said the woman on my left, to whom I had barely spoken up to that point, 'they're indoor sparklers. Charlotte told me.'

So we held our sparklers in the candle flames and lit them and chorused 'Happy Birthday' at the tops of our voices and held the sparklers aloft.

This was fine for the duration of the song – about twenty seconds – but I couldn't help noticing that, for indoor sparklers, these were awfully big. After about a minute, they were only half burned and the room was beginning to fill with black, sulphurous smoke. People were starting to look around anxiously, wondering where, behind the velvet drapes, the windows might be. There was a good deal of nervous laughter, accompanied by a lot of fanning and gesticulating. Some of the oldsters staggered to their feet and teetered towards the doors, while the more army-minded men grappled with the curtains and the sash windows behind them.

'Look,' said the woman to my left, hoarsely, 'those old ladies by the door . . . they've got bowls of water, *and they're breathing the water.*'

The sparklers were still going. I felt a hint of panic rising in my chest and wondered whether I should start to crawl out of the dining room at carpet level, wearing my napkin like a *chador*. To disguise my fear, I played with the packet the sparklers had arrived in.

'I'm sure they were meant to be for indoor use,' muttered my new friend, who clearly felt responsible in some way for the effect they were having. She took the packet from my numb fingers and looked at it. 'Oh,' she said. '"For Outdoor Use Only." Oh, dear.'

By now you couldn't see from one side of the room to the other. People were gagging furtively into their handkerchiefs. There was a kind of hysterical wartime gaiety as posh folk in their evening dresses wept and hacked and cackled with the mad, laugh-in-the-face-of-adversity absurdity of it all. *We're all going to die*, I thought, watching them chinning up and bearing it; *this Sloane's going to kill me.*

Then, suddenly, the windows were open and the last of the sparklers had gone out. Someone started to applaud, ironically. The men bravely straightened their ties and the women hefted themselves around inside their dresses. Everyone was looking around for casualties.

I essayed a heartless laugh. And then, as the capstone to the whole evening, the birthday cake came in, borne through the bitter fog which still remained by a couple of lackeys. And everyone started braying again as if nothing untoward had happened. Wiping their eyes and spitting and blowing their noses, they applauded the cake's arrival. They also applauded the fact that it was in the shape of a naked black man, with a fruit assortment made of icing covering his genitals.

Where, I wondered in all this, do they get their money from? Apart from Charlotte, who got hers from an assortment of dead relatives? How do these people manage to stay so well-heeled, so tinged with opulence? What do they do for a living?

Plainly, the first port of call is the City of London. Ever a byword for extremes of class-consciousness, the City used to divide neatly along the lines of upper class (who had the smart jobs in banks and broking firms) and working class (who were responsible for the trading side of things). There was a nicely nineteenth-century formality about this caste system, even allowing for the fact that the traders could earn more, sometimes, than their smart superiors. And indeed, much of that tone is still evident in modern class-ridden City life.

But things are changing. It's not so much that the City's contracting, denying itself to the kind of thick-witted Sloanes who would once have gone into the place without a moment's reflection (unlike the Army, which *is* shrinking; and never paid much, anyway); more that its emphases are shifting. A lot of the City is now owned by multinationals, cabals of puritannical Germans and Swiss, monomaniacal Americans. Barings have been snapped up by ING of Holland; Phillips & Drew disappeared into UBS of Switzerland long ago; Morgan Grenfell is owned by Deutsche Bank; even the great Warburg's have been swallowed up into the maw of the Swiss Bank Corporation; and of course, huge operators like Salomons' and Nomura were never English in the first place. And, much as they may enjoy the company of the Old Etonians and Harrovians, these foreign bosses only *really* like the ones who can make the figures add up satisfactorily.

The position was summed up by a grammar-school-boy-makes-good I met who worked for one of big, heavyweight internationals. He said that he had 'a couple of Etonians working under me. One of them's very bright, very good. The other one's as thick as pigshit. He just gets by on charm. He won't get very far.' And elsewhere? 'What's happening is that the not terribly clever extreme public-school types are still getting jobs in the City, but increasingly on the sales side, not on the board of directors. What they're good at is selling investments to rich old ladies over the phone. Or getting a job at Lloyd's, of course . . .'

As for the Sloanes and the socially advantaged who don't go to work in the City, their options seem to fall into two main categories: the smarmier professions; and small-time entrepreneurship. Thus, estate agency, the Bar, antiques dealing, flogging posh cars are all tolerable activities for anyone who wants to wear a suit or a twin-set and pearls to work. On the entrepreneurial side, things are more diverse, but still adhering to a general pattern. Little retailing businesses flogging wine, artificial flowers, knick-knacks, jewellery and whimsical trash are popular (you find them all over the charity gift fairs, as a matter of fact), as are food shops and, I am told, socially grand tupperware parties, in which posh women get other posh women into their houses and do a bit of pyramid selling. The most conspicuous kind of entrepreneurial activity involves clothes – shops like Pink's (the shirt-sellers), Hackett's (all-round fuddy-duddy gear) and a mail-order enterprise called Boden. This last was actually started by an ex-City broker called Johnnie Boden. His gag was to send out catalogues of tasty Sloane clothing actually modelled by his Sloane friends and acquaintances. The copy would be littered with names like Henry, Harriet, Hugh, Melissa, James. The burnished faces staring out would be dead-ringers for the society pages of *Tatler*, while posturing all the while in dressing-gowns and tasty flannel slacks.

Of course, some traditionalists go off and run estates or farm their family properties and buy *The Field*, while others (like the woman I overheard at the Eton v. Harrow match) are reduced to running B&Bs as a consequence of their own stupidity or negligence. But the mob at Charlotte's party? Essentially urban, essentially professional, essentially rolling in it.

★

Someone asked me if I'd been to Westminster School. I can't explain how this could have happened, except to suppose that the person who asked me must by then have been dead drunk, like me. It was the boy in white tie and tails who'd been attacked by the two fruity girls right at the start. The two girls, incidentally, were on the dancefloor (set up in the reception room while we ate). They were dancing so riotously with each other that one of them knocked the other one to the ground, where she rolled around in a tangle of knickers and lamé.

'Are you *sure* you weren't at Westminster?' said the boy. He was young, he was entitled to make a mistake. I tried to stop myself inflating too visibly. My cod voice reeled out of control. I laughed in what I hoped would pass for a mocking, relaxed fashion.

'Noah,' I drawled. 'I was – y'knoah – at 'nother place . . . hur, hur, hur . . .'

The boy was nonetheless impressed. I could tell. He leaned towards me. 'I think I'll be an MP in about fifteen years' time,' he said, very seriously.

I'd rather lost my grip on my eyebrows by this stage, but did my best to glance at him in a sage but interrogative manner, as someone might who regularly meets real and aspiring Tory politicians and knows how many beans make five.

'You see,' the boy went on, leaning uncertainly against the edge of a table, 'I was going to go to Blackpool' – for the Tory Party annual conference, in fact – 'but I thought, no. Better not. 'Cause I told my head of chambers that I wasn't interested in politics. He'd be bound to find out if I went up to Blackpool and he'd be really cross.'

I nodded assent at this wise decision. A barrister, too, eh? Did he ever go to a certain Tory dining club where people like Alan Clark get up to speak? I'd actually been to one the week before, and heard Alan Clark.

'Oh, *that*. Too stuffy.' He dismissed it with a wave of the palm. 'Do you know the Cresta Run people? The ones who slide down staircases on a silver tea tray? I know all of them.' He got me in focus and then lost me again. 'They're great fun. Met them at Oxford. I was very big in OUCA, [the Oxford University Conservative Association] and I've also got lifetime membership of Stringfellow's! I was there last night with a pretty girl and he let me in straight away! Then we left Stringfellow's and found a drinking club and I went to bed at six o'clock and got up at five o'clock this afternoon . . . in time for *Baywatch*! Ha, ha, ha, ha!'

At this point, the two girls who'd attacked him at the beginning of the party turned up again. By now, I was recklessly impersonating a Sloane – indeed, I'd been practising my impersonation on and off for several weeks, and the imposture just sprang horribly out, more or less unbidden. I leaned on the table top, genial but heavy-lidded, a cig perched between my fingers (not having smoked for ten years, I had started again, intermittently, to show that, far from being a middle-class prig, I was as heedless of my health as anyone) saying *yah* and *no, rilly* in a manner that was relaxed to the point of narcosis. What's more, I had been growing my hair so that it flopped around untidily; I had stopped myself straightening books and newspapers about the house, leaving them instead in random patterns where they lay; I drank more than was usual for me; I worked harder at getting out and about; I ate in a Vietnamese restaurant in Fulham, along with a lot of skinny teenage Sloane girls and their bovine boyfriends, and I tried not to try too hard. In short, I felt young and stupid again.

The two girls lurched into chairs beside Tails Boy. They'd known him all along, of course. The blonde one in the lamé dress started on about embarrassing dinner parties she'd been to. She'd just had dinner with another friend and a whole load of people and her boyfriend, and, '*everyone* there was a count or a Graf or whatever.'

'Oh, yah, *I* know,' said her friend in the black trousers.

'And right at the end, when everyone was totally drunk, at about two a.m., the girl who was *giving* the dinner party took out this visitors' book and said that we all had to sign it, *and* do a *drawing* in it, or *a picture* or something . . .'

Tails Boy and I did our best to shoot each other amused, tolerant glances.

'And I mean, the Queen Mother's actually been there, to dinner, apparently.'

'*Really?*'

'But apparently she didn't sign the visitors' book.'

'Well, she wouldn't, would she?'

'So of course, James' – the boyfriend – 'had to volunteer first, so they gave him a box of *watercolours* and a *brush*. And he spent ages trying to get the watercolours to go *on* the brush, but he'd forgotten that he needed some *water* first.'

'He's *so* sweet, James, *so* funny.'

Tails Boy and I rocked with mirth at this and groped for the wine bottle.

And then it suddenly became much more depraved. For a start, it seemed that a woman who was renting a bit of the black-trouser girl's flat was an ex-junkie coke fiend. One morning the cokehead had woken up, 'Then she did a line of coke and drank a whole bottle of sherry. Straight off.'

'*No!*'

'And then, in the afternoon, she threw up, all over the bathroom.'

'*No!*'

'I mean, she's *such* a liability.' The black-trouser girl took a tense suck at her cigarette. 'I'm going to have to get rid of her.'

I tried to intimate to everyone else that I wasn't a complete stranger to coke myself (a lie, unfortunately), and asked if they had

159

any more upper-class squalor to share with me. This sent Blondie into a spasm of social procuring (she must have assumed I was OK, because I seemed to be with Tails Boy and *he* was OK).

'I'll tell you who you've got to meet . . .'

'Who's that?' I replied, too eagerly.

'You should meet Julian.'

'Wow! Yah! Sure! Who's Julian?' It was like being at a teenage party. My social life was going to be something altogether else once I met Julian.

'Oh,' said Trousers, '*Julian's* just – oh, he's too much!'

There was a pause while Blondie looked at me through narrowed eyes. Then she decided to risk it and carry on anyway. 'Well, *Julian* . . . Julian used to run a porn-mag syndicate at Eton, 'cause he's absolutely *obsessed* with sex. I mean, he's got a really big chopper, apparently. He's supposed to be red hot in bed, as well—'

'I bet he doesn't rubber up,' interjected Trousers.

'Oh no, I think he always rubbers up.'

I stared at them uselessly for a moment. *Rubber up?*

'Wears a *condom*,' said Trousers. Despite myself, I ran a finger round the inside of my collar.

'Sure,' I lied.

'But anyway,' Blondie went on, clearly regretting the fact that she'd started on this particular piece of smut, 'he was at Annabel's with some other people, three boys, three girls, *and* . . .'

She leaned forward over the table. We all leaned forward. My eyes bulged.

'. . . and the girls did a line of coke off the guys' *dicks*.'

I made a noise like a damp paper bag bursting. Blondie thought I was being sceptical, when in fact I was merely being shocked.

'No they *did*,' she insisted. 'They all went to this dark corner of the club and put their dicks on the table and the girls did lines of coke off their *dicks*.'

I sat and glowed. Tails Boy had quiet hysterics and Trousers swatted him with her hand.

'It's *true!*' cried Trousers.

'Were you *there*?' shouted Tails Boy.

'No, but it's TRUE!' Blondie yelled back at him.

I flushed scarlet and crimson like a broken traffic-light and tried to puzzle it out. The darkened corner, the noise, pulling out your cock and trailing a line of white power on it. How would you keep it still? And why? And I was supposed to *meet* this person?

'Well, I'll give Julian a call, then,' I said.

As indeed I did: but I never met him. He answered the phone, Voice up full, and asked if I wanted to know about shooting. I said no, I wanted to know about the, er, high life. If he knew what I meant. He said, 'Oh, well, there's a bunch of us and we sort of go around together. Looking for girls, ha, ha! Young ones, usually, but older ones *if they wear the expensive underwear*, ha, ha, ha!' We arranged to get in touch, but it didn't happen. A mythical figure.

Then I found myself staring into the face of the sparklers woman. She'd been there all the time, having a conversation with another guest. To my surprise, she put her hand on my arm, and in a clear reference to Tails Boy, said, 'If I was a Tory MP's wife, I wouldn't let him shove *me* off into the country. I'd make sure I stayed in London.'

This was strange. Why were these people taking me into their confidence like this, unless they'd failed to rumble that I wasn't one of them? First Tails Boy, then Blondie and Trousers, and now, it seemed, the sparklers woman.

'A lot of the standard bankers and barristers are so shallow,' she went on.

I looked at her and frowned. She gave me a vatic nod.

The word 'acceptance' blinked in my mind with neon

persistence. True, the hostess Charlotte had barely addressed a word to me since I arrived, but then she was the birthday girl and had 129 more pressing guests to schmooze. And when I had lurched towards her with a 'shall-we-dance?' expression on my face, she had, essentially, walked straight past me. But apart from her, things didn't seem to matter nearly as much as I'd feared they would at the beginning. The sparklers woman was now limbering up to give me, her social co-equal, it seemed, her views on women's issues. It felt odd and unfamiliar and pleasant. After a few minutes of turgidities from Sparklers, I went and cut a deranged rug with the wife, bellowing 'yah' at her as often as I could. Was I having fun? Did I fit in?

A tall woman bound in green satin shouted at a boiling man, 'The next one's a fortieth, actually. It's going to be in Rules. And Hugo held a super forty-fifth birthday in the Reform Club. Which was terribly nice.'

What the hell, I decided. I might as well go all the way.

'Oh, the Reform's *super*,' I shouted back to the green satin woman, before bumping heavily into a wall. '*Super*.'

Clearly, things had changed in the weeks since Ascot and Cowdray Park. From being almost wholly excluded, I was now, very marginally, included . And – well what do you know? – I started to appreciate that smart people *do* have a use in society. And what might that be? Well, they're there to be both detestable and wretchedly appealing: objects of horrified fascination. People who invite our disapproval for almost everything they do, and thus answer a deep and ineradicable need in the rest of society to have someone else to envy, blame, loathe. Don't all societies have a layer of inadmissible privilege on the top? Certainly. But what makes the British version so perversely satisfying is that the top people are not only well-heeled, but their position in society is underpinned by a formal, codified class structure. It took me a long time to come to such an obvious conclusion, but I got there at last. As I said at the start, we're still living under an *ancien régime*. The thing is, we love these people.

And we love them because, unable to maintain continuity in any other part of our national existence, snobbery is the one thing we can hand down from generation to generation. We have no strategy for the new Europe; industry and commerce have somehow dribbled through our fingers and are either wholly-owned abroad, or dependent on overseas markets and investors; we have not a *clue* how to preserve the physical fabric of Britain, being content to let our towns fall to bits, our countryside disappear under chemical prairies, and the whole lot to sink under millions and millions of motor vehicles; we've no idea what democracy means anymore (a parliamentary autocracy, bolstered by quangos?). In other words, we've lost or are losing all the best of our past. Dimly conscious of this, but unable to do anything constructive about it, we cling to the one bit of the past we could actually do *without* as a kind of wretched palliative, a consolation for all the other things we've managed to throw away: we hang on to our Monarchy and all its attendant grandees and snobs.

We've done so all through this century – the century of Marx, the common man, universal suffrage, the Welfare State, you name it. We've always turned our gaze towards the upper classes, just to see what the bastards will get up to next. And we're secretly thrilled when they satisfy our dreams of what posh people ought to get up to. It's the diaries of James Lees-Milne all over again. It's Lord Howard of Effingham being bound over in 1929 after getting into a fight involving eighty people outside a nightclub. It's Lord Noel-Buxton attempting, in 1952, to walk across the Thames at Westminster in order to prove that an ancient ford existed there. The buffoon had to swim it, of course, arguing afterwards that, 'There was much more water than I expected. It must be all that rain up in the Cotswolds.' It's Sir Mark Palmer, former page to the Queen, being busted for drugs (we're in 1968, now), having his antique water pipe confiscated and driving off in a horse and trap while wearing a gold silk waistcoat and yellow velvet trousers. It's Fergie, having her toes sucked by her soon-to-be-declared-bankrupt financial adviser . . .

And it's why we read *Hello! Hello!*, of course, is the joker in the pack of posh-fixated mags. While *Harpers, Tatler* and the rest give the impression of being produced by posh people for posh people (with us, the mob, fortuitously sneaking in for a quick gander), *Hello!* (with a circulation of 476,000 – nearly three times that of the other two combined) is nakedly downmarket. And as such, it depicts its posh victims in a manner which is both fawning and vicious. There's a literal, reductive quality to the pictures which tends to make them look like pornography or the illustrations out of a medical textbook. The mechanically grovelling prose only heightens the sense of ironic victimisation, like Goldberg and McCann softening up Stanley in *The Birthday Party*. And the message of *Hello!* – the glaring subtext, to be honest – is that we actually sanction these people to behave as unreasonable, unprincipled, overprivileged snobs. As long as they do so, they justify their own existence. (Posh people read *Hello!*, of course, because they want the gossip as much as the rest of us. But they read *Debrett's* as well, in an effort to synthesise some kind of philosophical understanding of their place in the world. At first I didn't believe that anyone read *Debrett's*, but I was subsequently told of at least three families whose idea of a good night in is to sit down – like Sir Walter Elliot in *Persuasion* – and look themselves and their collaterals up in the *Peerage & Baronetage*.)

This was why I was so fevered at the prospect of attending the Sloane's birthday party in Kensington. In the great scheme of things – in comparison with 'Jennifer's Diary', for instance – it was nothing, barely an event. But from my dingy perspective, it was a thrilling taste of that deplorable world from which I had felt myself wholly excluded for so long. That's why I was so exercised by the boy who thought I'd been to Westminster. That's why I was agog at the revelations of the Blondie and Trousers, the two society party girls. That's why I felt such a degree of vertigo when Mrs Teeth and I nearly had a conversation about Harry the Scottish dancing instructor. I felt as if I had escaped my bourgeois condition for those fleeting seconds and was almost . . . one of *them*.

EIGHT

Well, now. This was a turn-up. This was the last thing I'd legislated for: that I might actually *enjoy* myself. I'd started off at Ascot, comfortable in the knowledge that whatever else posh people were, they weren't justifiable, whereas I was. I'd nurtured my detestation through polo, the great boys' boarding schools, Queen Charlotte's Ball, Scottish dancing lessons and the Henley Regatta. I'd hated the English class system, with the Queen at its apex, its entrenched social structures in finance, industry and so on – anything which, to my way of thinking, rendered this country backward, inefficient and unfair. I'd kept myself appalled at all times. Why the fuck (it came down to this) should I defer to anyone else just because their father left them a title? Or because they went to a heavy-hitting school which taught them how to cut people like me dead? Or because they could somehow prey on the old English morbid class sensibilities?

And yet, at the far end of my trawl through what I imagined

posh to be, I'd forgotten about being angry. I was worrying instead about how I could get some more of this life. It was getting suspiciously like my bad spell after a year at Oxford – the silverware and claret period, the 'yah' period – all over again. A token rub-up, and I was no longer dull Mr Suburban; I was Mr Pinchbeck Socialite, the impostor from the sticks.

And when the time came for me to go on my mid-winter shoot, I actually found myself, not exactly looking forward to it, but at least anticipating it with a strange keenness. It wasn't as if I *liked* what I was doing; I just *wanted* it, in the way that one succumbs to any unhealthy addiction. I was ambivalently waiting to pleasure myself. I was so filled with dubious anticipation, in fact, that I nobbled a chap called Hugh who'd been to the Royal Agricultural College at Cirencester. I wanted to get some tips off him about rural life and bucolic practices before going out with my new smart friends. As it turned out, he wanted to talk about confusion rather than farming: but that, in itself, was all right with me.

'Only about one person a year died when I was a Cirencester,' he began, matter-of-factly snorting a Pale Ale in this tweedy London pub. 'Usually trying to get to the ton.'

You have to go to Cirencester to get the full measure of what he was talking about. The Royal Agricultural College sits in a big patch of mud and grass on the outskirts of the town (an extremely salubrious Cotswold market town: old, honeyed stone, lovely church, dear little traffic-choked streets, branch of the General Trading Company, other shops unchanged from the 1950s unaffectedly selling Barbours and headscarves; Tetbury, Highgrove, the Royals etc. all within easy reach).

The main building is Victorian Gothic, a little bit Balliol, a little bit Oxford University Museum, a little bit Munster family. And there is a very long, dead straight drive leading from the main road to the front door. For years, what you had to do, if you were a well-connected, flannel-brained agricultural student, was start your MG or your motorbike at one end of the drive, hit 100mph about two thirds of the way along, and successfully come to a halt at the other end before you crashed into the building. That was the idea.

When Hugh was up, doing his course, various people had a go, but bottled out before reaching the magic ton. In an MG, of course, you'd be lucky to reach 60. But on a motorbike, it was different.

'One guy claimed to have done it,' said Hugh, knitting his brows, 'but he didn't have anyone riding pillion to corroborate. So another guy had a go, with someone riding pillion.'

Didn't it occur to him that, with another large person on board, the bike might not have been able to accelerate quickly enough? Hugh frowned a bit and considered this idea as if it were new to him. This gave me time to admire his wonderfully cut chalk-stripe suit and his silk tie and his glinting black half-brogues; and to nurture a shallow but painful envy for his material good fortune (got into estate agency after Cirencester).

'What he did,' Hugh went on eventually, 'was leave his braking too late. He went straight up the steps, through the main doors, smashed them down, killing two people on the other side, went up the stairs, still on the bike with the guy riding pillion, hit the window at the top of the stairs and went through it. He and the passenger hit the bottom of the courtyard below, where they were both killed.'

This is ghastly, of course, dreadful. But then, about ten or twenty years ago, this is what you did at Cirencester. The place must have been almost entirely populated by people for whom the idea of study, as a pursuit in itself, would have been un-intelligible. The idea was mainly to go mad but also to get a qualification at the end. Think of it: you take a large number of demented Sloane men, stick them in a field, give them unlimited access to drink, motor vehicles and each other's company for anything between one and three years. All students like to combine business and pleasure, of course, but given the unusually narrow social composition of the average Cirencester intake (people about to inherit land, run someone else's inherited land, or just deal on a day-to-day basis with hard-core heirs and landowners), the whole thing must have been about as far removed from the conventions of learning as a weekend with Lana Turner.

'Everyone,' according to my new friend Hugh, 'used to come in for the first lecture on Monday morning with the most *appalling* hangovers. If they made it in at all.'

Life for Hugh and his friends was clearly an intentional shambles, intermittently ordered by such signposts as exams, overdrafts, death, car breakdowns, arrest, pub-opening times, girlfriends' arrivals and departures. People wrote up their lecture notes in pubs (a Bloody Mary, an A4 pad, the Wild Duck at Ewen), caught up on their sleep in lectures, worked hard at their fox-hunting, drove off the road, did their reading in the lavatory, covered themselves in mud, got lost on the M4, woke up in houses which were not theirs, mislaid all their personal possessions, arrived pathetically early or insultingly late, but never at the right time, and wore each other's clothes without meaning to.

'Oh, yah! We used to wear each other's clothes all the time!'

We were back to the good old days.

'We're all from the same set, basically. Think the same way, dress the same. And people who were the same height would always wear each other's clothes. You'd see a sweater, put it on and the next day, someone would say, "I've got a sweater just like that!" And you'd say, "Yes! It's yours!"'

What a bunch you must have been!

'Oh, the *real* problem was when you'd grab a Barbour — 'cause they all look the same — put it on to go out to a lecture in the field, feel around in the pocket for your pen, realise you'd put on someone else's coat and hadn't *got* a pen, so you wouldn't be able to take any notes! Ha, ha, ha!'

Well, *bingo!* I thought to myself. Of *course*. Confusion, muddle, chaos: that's what's so socially smart. It's that denial of the bourgeois essentials, priorities, categories of being, which provides the clincher, once you've dealt with education, voice and seasonal activities.

Look at this way: when posh people throw a charity fest, what do they do? Turn it into a drinks party. When they have a ball, what do they do? Pretend it's for charity. When they live almost entirely for themselves, what do they do? Harp on about their greater obligations to society. When they go to some of the finest schools in the land, what do they do? Narrow their horizons almost to vanishing point. When they buy a terrific old house in the country, full of beautiful furnishings, what do they do? Allow it to cover itself in grime and ordure, because cleaning things is middle-class. What do they do with their expensive, well-tailored clothes? Get dog hairs on them, bag the pockets, muddle them up with their shitty old gardening clothes and leave them on the floor. When do they talk most? When they haven't got anything to say. What do they say when they've got something important to communicate? Nothing. When do they try their hardest to have fun? When they're working. What do they work hardest at? Having fun. Life, in short, is arranged along the lines of a high-tone jumble sale, a muddle of precious activities and obsessions. And this derangement of priorities is vital in setting the right tone — enabling the posh to be so careless, so *fuck-you*, so dismissive.

Middle-class people like me prefer to keep things tidy. Tidiness is the middle-class vice. We clean our cars, we hoover our floors, we attach one set of values to the world of work and another to leisure, we tend to be boringly moralistic about things, neatly and persistently attributing rightness and wrongness to events and actions, we spend a fortune on lavatory products, we have hierarchies of worthwhile and unworthwhile activities, we have hobbies. The middle classes have a monopoly on neurosis, and neurosis is all about the demented pursuit of order and control, practised by people who essentially feel that everything is contingent and could fall apart at any minute. The middle classes have, if you like, got as far as anal retention, while posh people are still orally fixated.

(This, incidentally, throws up another upper-class confusion. It's always quite clear to me when another middle-class person is about to go bonkers: they can't cope, they can't order their lives, they give every indication of being about to go bats. But the majority of posh people I've come across – Sloanes, Etonians, the lot – have seemed to me to be stark mad most of the time, without it affecting their capacity to deal with their world.)

I know there's a common parallel drawn between the upper classes and what used to be known as the working classes; that both groups have a similarly *carpe diem* approach to life. Both play hard, smoke, are unencumbered by snotty bourgeois proprieties and are a good deal more relaxed about sexual promiscuity, drink, gambling, divorce, violence, and so on. Which is why, of course, horse races are full of one social group or the other, but less frequented by conscientious, fucked-up, bourgeois types.

But I would claim that this admittedly old-hat, sentimental view of things omits one great difference: that the old working classes still went about their business one thing at a time. You worked your nuts off (when you worked), and then you kept pigeons or read Karl Marx or pleasured yourself, in the vein of Albert Finney with Rachel Roberts in *Saturday Night and Sunday Morning*. And if you were Bryan Pringle, and you discovered that your wife, played by Rachel Roberts, was being tupped by Albert Finney, you took time out to make sure he got his face stamped on. You didn't try to do it while putting a deal together or throwing a dinner party. You compartmentalised your life, in other words. You didn't try to turn everything into an hilarious mishmash.

But if you're posh, a shambles, a mish-mash, is precisely what you want. And you want it even if it means that you end up acting like a delinquent or a cretin. It's like the grandee woman who (according to an eyewitness) was at a ball, went off for a pee, came back and danced around for ten minutes oblivious to the fact that she'd tucked the back of her ballgown down her knickers. It's the superannuated lord I once met in a merchant bank, who'd been given the job of liaising with the hacks. His manners were impeccable, his suit was hand-made but covered in food, and he hadn't got a clue where he was in the building. The secretaries kept having to tell him where the lifts were. It's the super-smart county woman in a London restaurant who enjoyed her meal so much that, after looking around when she'd finished to check that the coast was clear, picked up her plate and licked it clean. It's the Rugby-educated stockbroker who got pissed one night after work, got on the last train home to Kent, fell asleep, woke up in Folkestone at midnight, decided to sober up by buying himself a round trip on the cross-Channel ferry, had a few drinks on the ferry, got to France, decided he'd sober up better if he took a round trip on the train to Paris, got to Paris, decided he liked it so much that he'd spend a couple of days there and got home four days late to find his wife filing for divorce.

★

Times change, of course, even at Cirencester Agricultural College. Everybody takes things more seriously. Women study there now, and that in itself brings sobriety and singlemindedness to the proceedings. Moreover, jobs on the great estates aren't a giveaway these days, no matter how well connected you may be. Titled employers may even look to see what sort of grade you got in your final exams. And doing 100mph down the main drag has been outlawed: but not before another bright spark had the idea of turning the dare on its head, starting at the front door, and driving as fast as he could, out on to the main road.

'Now that was a real wheeze! He started at the entrance to the building in his car, and got his friends, with CB radios, to hold up the traffic on the road [this is the A433 to Bath, incidentally, a really busy highway] in case he couldn't stop in time. There was a field on the other side of the road and a hedge, so he thought, if I can't stop, at least I'll just run into a hedge and I won't damage the car too much.'

Good idea! I cried, entering into the spirit of things. So he did the magic ton?

'Oh, it worked perfectly. He went flat out, they stopped the traffic, he couldn't stop in time and shot across the road.'

And?

'Well, he forget that immediately opposite the entrance to the college there is a wooden telegraph pole, and he drove straight into it. Totalled the car. He was all right, though. The telegraph pole's still leaning over at an angle where he hit it.'

This is true. At the time of writing, the pole was definitely listing. I went to have a look.

Hugh burbled on.

'Then everybody used to drive *over* the roundabout at the entrance to Cirencester, over the grass bit in the middle, instead of

173

going round it, and the police put up a big reflective barrier to stop them. So this chap went out at two in the morning with his shotgun and blasted the barrier with pellets. You can still see the holes. I think they arrested him. Another beer?'

Was the birthday party solely responsible for my change of mood? Was it the experimental glass of Dr Harris's Pick-Me-Up which I had the day after? (This is a tonic which you buy from an awesomely olde-worlde chemist's shop in St James's Street. It's By Appointment to the Queen Mother, who lives just at the end of the road. It describes itself as 'a splendid reviver in the morning' and tastes like a great draught of public lavatories.)

And why should this have surprised me? Smart muddle has a lot going for it. It's anti-intellectual, hedonistic, sentimental, slovenly. All the things one would like to be, given a break from the nagging obligations of a middle-class upbringing. Why, for instance, was it such a lark to visit Princess Diana's very own gym, the Harbour Club, in West London, which I also squeezed in before my shoot? Because it demonstrates such a lush, beguiling, upper-class confusion of priorities.

Up to this point, the only health clubs I'd ever visited had been smelly, monomaniacal places lit by cruel, unsympathetic lights: dungeons of the self, where wild-eyed women in leotards and bitter executives punished themselves on the off-chance of rescheduling their cardiac infarctions. The mood was always relentless, dour, literal. At the Harbour Club, by way of contrast, there was a selection of stony-faced but quintessentially indolent Sloane women and track-suited media lizards, tippling away at Bloody Marys and hauling on Silk Cuts and Marlboro Lights. There was also a huge bar, stocked with beer, wine, vodka, whisky, and a menu offering eggs Florentine and bread and butter pudding.

Indeed, in the evenings (I was told) the place bulks out dramatically with unattached merchant bankers and Chelsea women who hang around talking and drinking and smoking, treating the place purely as a hyper-exclusive wine bar (£12,000 just to join), and barely looking at the costly rowing machines and treadmills downstairs. It is a health club for the socially smart, because it is all about eating and drinking and smoking and having *fun*. Ideologically, it is a shambles.

Indeed, the gracious Sloane lady who'd taken me in there with her friend generated a perfect confusion of her own. We sat down in the Philippe Starck-ish interior (splashes of acid colour, retro knowingness, tiresome ironies) and the Sloane lady chose a glass of water and a salad. The friend ordered herself a self-denying Bloody Mary and had a cigarette, while I had a beer and an egg. Fine, I thought – it is a health club. The Sloane lady clearly wanted to keep the faith. But about halfway through the meal, such as it was, she suddenly snapped, ordered a bottle of Chablis, some bread and butter pudding, and started bumming fags off me like a teenager. At the time, I found this such a breathtaking inversion of the conventions of health-club life, it was positively Dada.

Then I underwent a small apotheosis during my shoot. There it was: the last item on my *Book of the Season* list, and time to part company with Lady Celestria Noel ('There may be the odd lucky person who gets enough shooting . . . through charm, ability, sucking up, etc. . . .'). Bearing in mind that it costs around £40 a bird to shoot grouse and £17 a bird to shoot pheasant, I did wonder if this last jaunt wasn't going to bankrupt me – but of course I wasn't allowed to wield a gun. Far too dangerous. Instead, I was graciously allowed to stagger around for hours on end, acting as a beater. And it was *fine*. I was so inured, by now, to being in the company of the posh that I'd simply lost the capacity to take offence. Looking back, I realise that the whole thing should have driven me mad with rage: about twenty county Sloanes stumbling around the Buckinghamshire countryside, braying and mooing and shooting wildly at birds and laughing their fuck-you laughs. But it didn't.

For a start, it was a beautiful winter's morning when we met. It was very cold, very bright, everything covered in a dazzling blanket of frost. The benign Buckinghamshire hills rolled away into a pale blue haze. The sun hung in a brilliant empyrean. We stood around in this farmer's courtyard, stamping our feet and puffing and blowing to keep ourselves warm, while some very *Horse and Hound* dogs scampered after smells. There were eight guns and twelve beaters – the beaters being friends and relations, rather than bitterly monosyllabic professional gillies.

And that was the second thing: the relative modesty of the whole event. Until I was invited on this particular shoot, I'd been trying to work my way on to a shoot on one of the Duke of Buccleuch's estates. This, I was led to believe, would have been a big-scale, heavily pro meeting – lots of money around, real beaters, everyone banging away in a deeply competitive manner on an enormous piece of land in Northamptonshire.

But then my home-counties event turned up, and it was clear from the start that it was going to be far more domestic in scale. The area being covered was only a few acres; the guns were all being wielded by the local squirearchy, rather than a lot of pretentious City types. The beaters included goofy teenage girls, moon-faced young men, implacable Sloane wives and one very old whiskery man covered from head to foot in oilskins, who had apparently been a poacher for most of his life. He was hugely impressive, looking as he did like a cross between Mr Chips and

176

a hedgehog. When someone demanded that we should all take part in a group photo, the whiskery ex-poacher said, 'Do-yer-flies-up time, eh?' and went off into a wheezy cackle behind a gorse bush. The atmosphere was breezily informal, and the farmer on whose land the shoot was taking place was, frankly, everything you could want in a farmer in Buckinghamshire: red-faced, genial, talkative, hands the size of baseball mitts, perfectly hopeless with a gun, a bit county for everyday use but, in context, absolutely OK.

The shooting syndicate was actually run by a tall, thin chap whom everyone called Stephenson. I never found out his first name. He stood and read out some bluff notes while we waited to go off and kill things. The guns could shoot pheasants (which had been reared for this purpose), partridges (which hadn't), foxes, magpies and crows.

'If your mobile goes off,' Stephenson went on, 'there's a twenty-pound fine. Fifty pounds if you answer it.'

A flutter of laughter went through the party, particularly from a large Sloane boy who'd turned up in a spanking new Golf GTi ('Yah, it's got sixteen vees,' I overheard him telling his friends, proudly), who clearly had at least one mobile phone about him, and maybe two. Then we all stumped off to look for some animals to shoot.

I was glad to see that it was going to turn into another confusion of purposes: a mish-mash of work, pleasure, exercise, bestial instinct. Up to now, I hadn't appreciated that going out with some people and banging away at things was anything other than a way of passing the time in winter. Could be clay pigeons, could be the real thing, I supposed. Just something moving that you could blow out of the sky.

But this kind of shooting is actually part foraging for food, part sport, part rural housekeeping, part social opportunity. The pheasants are reared until they're about four weeks old, then released in August to feed themselves up in time for the start of the pheasant-shooting season in October. Then, the idea is to shoot them, cook them and eat them. The fact that good shots usually kill far more birds than they want, or can stuff in their chest freezers, is an accident of human nature.

At the same time, your landowner gets a few pests, of the fox and magpie variety, cleared off his property, the better to protect his crops or his chickens or whatever. There is, in other words, a purely utilitarian component to the activity; particularly on a small-scale home counties shoot, where you may actually be lending a neighbourly hand to one of your farming colleagues. It's not *quite* like the great days of the Edwardian shooting party, when millions of pointlessly dead birds were strung up as mere trophies for a rabble of gun-mad toffs.

(Incidentally, I once went to see the film *The Shooting Party*, in which James Mason, Edward Fox and Dorothy Tutin all wear smart Edwardian clobber and go out in 1913 and slaughter some creatures, thus prefiguring the Great War. It was at the Curzon cinema, Mayfair – the one where Lady Bridget Parsons had fallen asleep next to James Lees-Milne – and there was a good Mayfair crowd in to watch a film dealing with something that they actually knew a bit about. One chap in the audience waited until a slow part of the movie before shouting out, 'Damn feller's holding his gun wrong.')

You also need a dog. There was a mixed bag of mutts chasing around in that witless way that dogs do. Three of them were apparently Hungarian pointers – slim, russet-coloured, nervously intelligent-looking. One of the beaters had seen a pointer in action before and spent a long time trying to persuade the rest of us that they really live up to their billing: 'I couldn't believe it!' he cried, fixing me with a mad stare. 'I saw one standing right over a bird which was acting dead on the ground two feet away, and it was pointing! The dog was actually pointing at it!'

The host farmer took a different view. As we marched over the frosty ground, he was busy explaining the minutiae of gun ownership ('a decent English-made gun's about £1,600') and the reasons why so many farmers commit suicide ('terribly lonely business, these days'), before launching into a hymn of praise to the spaniel.

'Now, a spaniel's a very good dog,' he said, pointing at a deranged mutt trying to jam its head under a bush. 'Very diligent. It'll go through anything after a bird. Gorse, nettles – anything.'

This was echoed by an old diesel who was one of the beaters. 'Wonderful dogs, spaniels,' she rasped, taking a B&H out of her mouth. 'Go into it like a bullet. They've only got to see something, and whoosh! They're straight in.' Then she stopped and looked angrily at me. 'Have you got a stick?' she demanded. I patted my pockets and shrugged. 'Well, you'll need a stick,' she barked. 'Better get yourself one.'

I soon found out why you need a stick if you're a beater. You use it to hit things with. About half an hour after we left the farm buildings, we found ourselves standing in a thicket of gorse, teasels, brambles and saplings in their protective plastic sleeves. This is where the twelve beaters stationed themselves, milling around in about an acre of frost-laden undergrowth; while the guns stood a few hundred yards away, staring hopefully into the air. The woman who'd told me to get a stick (I found one in a ditch, incidentally: a great, half-rotten piece of branch which flew into pieces the moment I struck it against anything) turned out to be in charge and was angrily trying to co-ordinate the beaters with the guns.

'Normally,' she growled, 'Roger pinches a couple of walkie-talkies from work on Friday night and gives them back on

Monday. And we communicate with the guns by walkie-talkie. But he hasn't done that today. So it's not as well organised as it might be. ARE YOU BLOODY READY YET?'

There was a faint hooting noise from the guns.

'I can't hear a bloody thing,' she muttered. 'Oh, let's just assume they're ready. Stop them dozing. ALL RIGHT EVERYONE, SPREAD OUT!'

We spread out as bidden and started to march through the wet, bristly mass of the thicket, shouting and thrashing as we went. It was like being back at school again, embarking on some fat-headed special project, the gym master bellowing at us from over the brow of a hill. The main difference was that I was stumbling through the vegetation in a cloud of scent, left in a vapour trail by the expensive wives and daughters of the guns in the next field. Once in a while, a pheasant would burst from the ground, with that frantic mechanical threshing noise they seem to make. And on one occasion, we startled a thing that looked like a pig covered in fur from its hide. 'Muntjac,' said a boy beater, sagely. 'There's lots round here. Escaped from Woburn, probably.'

Let's be honest, what better way is there to spend a crisp, clear, winter's morning than a hearty walk and a spell of physical exercise? 'I love beating,' announced a woman in a large trilby hat and a pair of brand-new Timberland boots. 'I love doing it with the professional beaters, too. They're so rude about the guns.'

We threshed on a bit more. Someone said they were feeling the cold. The hat-and-boots woman peeled off into a reminiscence.

'This is cold,' she averred, 'but nothing like Northumberland.'

'Oh, Northumberland can be *terribly* cold,' agreed a young female beater.

'We were up there,' the hat-and-boots woman went on, flattening a sapling with her walking stick, 'and we had a dance on Saturday and shooting on Friday and it was *so* cold. I've never been so cold. It was this horizontal hail blowing off the North Sea.' She chopped down a bush. 'Of course, they do know how to throw a dance in Northumberland . . .'

The guns, meanwhile, were either banging away frantically in all directions or completely silent, waiting for us to start the beating which – they'd failed to realise – we'd already begun five minutes earlier. The pheasants had learned to jump up from the ground and either fly towards the guns so low that the guns couldn't risk firing at them (because they'd end up firing at each other), or rocket vertically upwards and then fly straight over the beaters' heads, in the direction from which the beaters had just come. They would then settle down in the already-beaten undergrowth and go to sleep. It took us about eight drives to bag twenty-five birds. Our host didn't hit a single one, but he seemed happy enough.

'At least the weather's good,' he said bracingly. 'Last weekend it was just pouring. I've never been so depressed.'

And then we piled off for lunch.

This is the thing, isn't it? This is what you do. A modicum of hardish, useful-ish work, lovely surroundings, a bit of slaughter, then back indoors, shoes off (about half the men were standing around steaming unselfconsciously in their extra-thick hiking socks), drink in hand and the prospect of a really first-rate beef stew to contemplate. Logs crackled in the grate; the winter sun began to cast blue shadows across the fields outside. Everyone drank a few more snorts and then jollied themselves around the table. It was so apparently benign that I just sank uncritically into it. Twisted perceptions after eight months of hanging around smart types? Drink? Whatever it was, nothing could puncture my sense of unresisting complacency. Not even when one of the guns (a fat geezer in a Tattersall-check shirt, plus fours and tank-like brogues) slurped his wine after the main course and started musing on the idle life.

'My grandfather and my uncle inherited huge sums of money. Never worked from one end of their lives to another. Just amused themselves. Of course, by the time they died, there was nothing left. They'd frittered it all away.'

He took another gulp.

'I actually know one or two people who still do that. Just amuse themselves.'

'Don't they ever get bored?' I asked, before he slipped into unconsciousness.

'No,' he said, gazing rheumily at me. 'I don't think they're bright enough to get bored.'

A bloke next to him, with bouffant black hair, then started to reminisce about someone or other who was also stupid.

'You know why he got that job in mining?' asked Mr Hair. Everyone shook their heads helpfully. I shook my head, too. 'He meant to go into marketing, but he ticked the wrong box! Ticked mining instead of marketing! But they liked the cut of his jib and sent him anyway.'

How we roared! And how I roared, too. I didn't roar, I have to say, when Mr Hair later attempted his notorious impersonation of Archbishop Desmond Tutu. This was after a bit of prompting from his wife – or at least, a woman who seemed to know him quite well.

'Go on, Johnny,' she cried, 'you haven't done your Desmond Tutu yet!'

Doing Desmond Tutu, it transpired, consisted of Johnny sitting low in his chair and saying 'Tutu! Tutu!' in a piping cod Afrikaans.

'Oh, that's terribly good!' said a baldie at the end of the table.

'Tutu! Tutu!' chirruped Johnny/Hair, sliding lower and lower in his chair. He looked and sounded like a great, red-faced bird crested with black, as he sank almost out of view. The table rocked with merriment.

'Tutu!' he cheeped again, before mirth got the better of him.

Now, shouldn't I have made a protest here? Shouldn't I have pointed out that the Archbishop was a Nobel Prize-winner, heroic campaigner against the injustices of apartheid, a great-souled human being? What did I think I was doing? What happened to my cherished liberal intelligentsia values? If this didn't make me take offence, what would?

Obviously, a mixture of good manners (they were giving me a day out and a free meal) and cowardice (there were lots of them, and they were typically hefty in build) prevented me from making an issue of it. But on top of that, I'd guiltily realised how seductive it is to be reactionary; to be a muddle-headed, pleasure-seeking conservative. I realised how nice it must be to worry about frivolous things, and to be frivolous about serious things. And to have the number and nature of the things I could worry about strictly limited and defined: sniffing coke off penises, Harry's Scottish dancing classes, Ascot drill – these were the things to bother with; rather than those staples of middle-class *angst* – injustice, world poverty and the technological dystopia. After all, as Evelyn Waugh said, becoming a gentleman 'is essentially a process of ruling *out*'. For God's sake, I'd even talked myself into approving of bloodsports (on the basis, mainly, that since I cheerfully eat battery chickens raised in conditions of the most abominable squalor and cruelty, I wasn't really in a position to have a go at free-range pheasants, however caught). And besides, I argued to myself as Johnny/Hair did his Tutu, this kind of reactionary banter was less personally obnoxious than, say, the Tory dining club I had infiltrated, and where I had heard Alan Clark speak, and which had made such a pitiful impression on Tails Boy.

Just to clear things up: this dining club was a mixture of tittering Nazis and Oxbridge debating-society types. Viz: a bald, pop-eyed fellow sitting opposite me averred at one point that without a monarch as the head of state, the British Army would sit down and refuse to fight.

'They wouldn't fight for some wishy-washy load of politicians,' he said with some heat. 'They fight for *Queen* and *country*. If you asked them to abandon the monarch, they'd *snap* their *swords*.' He looked accusingly at me. 'I was in the Army,' he said, by way of explanation. 'For a short time. Hyar! Hyar!'

This last was what I recognised as the Oxford Debating Laugh: what pricks at Oxford – pricks in itchy tweed jackets and beetle-crusher brogues, generally – used to do as an exercise in debating. The routine is to adopt a particularly idiotic or offensive *épater-les-bourgeois* intellectual posture, expound it shamelessly, then leven the whole thing with a rattle of nasal laughter, to suggest that they're so cynically brilliant that they can sustain twenty minutes of freely associative crap, whether they believe it or not.

But the real luxury that he and his fellow-members enjoyed was the luxury of conservative, anti-progressive, teak-headed thought. It was the ebb and flow of hard-core reactionary apothegms and Little Englander platitudes that kept them so young, so buoyant. What can it be like, I wondered, as Clark spoke and an evil-tempered cleric next to me kept farting and picking his filthy fingernails, to hold to a reactionary view of the world all the time? Nothing to worry about, no complexities or ambiguities. Just the decline of Britain and society, largely as the result of pernicious foreigners, trades unions and state schooling. Why worry about class structures? Why worry about economic efficiency or fairness? Why worry about the next century? At least Johnny/Hair wasn't *that* bad.

All that remained of my moral sense by now was a desire to

make a great play of busying myself with the Stilton, so that I wouldn't be seen not laughing. But even as I felt myself being corrupted by experience, another beefy character in a pair of twill trousers was baring his soul: 'We've lost our toys, you see,' he said plaintively. 'We know we're just little boys really, and we want our toys back.'

I gave up and let it all wash over me. It had been a long day. Soon the huntsmen and their women were back on track. They were busying themselves with holiday tales, Henley anecdotes, balls, Christmas house parties, the proper substance of a posh life. I concentrated on eating as much as I could and beaming at them.

But who did I think I was kidding? A few days after my shoot, I sobered up. I realised that I would never have been asked without a reason. 'Oh, you're writing a book. You must come along.' I was just a tourist. They were showing me a few tribal customs, safe in the certainty that I was never going to come back again. Not long after my happy day with the pheasants, Prince Edward claimed in an interview: 'We are always being told that we have a rigid class structure. That's a load of codswallop.' How, one wonders, would *he* know? Had he spent a day with *me*?

I knew where I stood the moment I turned up at the wedding – the one I mentioned at the beginning of the book. The one in the grounds of the vast eighteenth-century house in Dorset. The one where everyone there was in a morning suit, except for me, in my chainstore threads. The one where the woman in green had been at school with Princess Diana. The one where there was a relatively tiny social distance between us which amounted to a chasm. The one where I was, basically, Mr Salteena all over again, at the wedding of Ethel Monticue and Bernard Clark: 'Mr Salteena all in black and looking bitterly sad and he ground his teeth.' Having got so far, I was reminded that I really hadn't got anywhere at all.

Without a doubt, it gave things a nice circularity, if you like: from Ascot bum to blithe social conman and back again. But there was nothing much to be said for nice circularity as I stood in the line to pay my respects to the bride and groom, and was handed a shot glass of ginger liqueur to warm me up by a flunkey whose perceptible hesitation when he saw me made me feel that I was in danger of being sent off to enjoy the rest of the event in the kitchens. I had no real purchase on my place in society.

I was not, to use the Sloane acronym, PLU – People Like Us. I was People Like Me. And the worst of it was that it mattered. (How, indeed, did I get invited in the first place? Sheer, Koestleresque coincidence. A friend turned out to be marrying a posh bloke. Nice people, really. But was I brought along simply to make up the numbers? In my gratitude at being invited, it didn't occur to me that I might feel like a freak, a pariah.)

When the woman in green started on about the *Sun*'s Pandora's Box of revelatory royal photographs, I tried to cheer myself by thinking of how soon it would be before the monarchy was exposed for the incontinent fraud it actually is (much as we can now read, fifty years after the event, that the Duchess of Windsor was a man and that Edward VIII only married him because he knew the black art of preventing premature ejaculation by means of what is known as the Singapore Grip), and of how then the edifice of class structure in England would take its cue from the House of Windsor and gradually dwindle and fall. One day things might be so advanced as to resemble the state of affairs currently existing in France or Germany. The impossible feudalities and condescensions of today's constitutionally sanctioned arrangements will vanish like the smell of stale drink. And then we will bask in the bright sunshine of a fresh, transparent, cash-based class system that has as its elite only successful entrepreneurs and Lottery winners.

But I didn't feel cheered. Only part of me went along with my own propaganda. The other part sat next to the green woman and made me wish that I too could be a perversely charming, born-and-bred, gregarious, tiny-minded Sloane like her and all her friends.

I had to put a stop to all this nonsense. There were incontrovert-ible truths, and one of them was that I could no longer stand being around posh people. It was becoming a slow and, frankly, expensive, torture. I got a grip on myself. I took charge. First, I put away my dinner jacket and my cheap suit and my Henley outfit at the back of the wardrobe. Then I inspected my face in the mirror. As I thought: no hint of classy in-breeding; none of that quality which allows you to look at the current Duchess of Slag and compare her with her ancestors – as painted by Lely or Reynolds – and say, 'My God! The genetic inheritance!'; or 'Wow! Breeding sure does tell!' None of that grand physiognomy . . . women with faces like dogs, cows, horses; men looking like old wallets, crumbling masonry, overripe fruit and veg, etc. Just a face of the suburbs, a bit pink and jowlly, nothing remarkable at all. And finally, I binned my *Harpers & Queen Book of the Season*. I looked at the picture of Lady Celestria Noel on the back, as if to say goodbye and thank you. She stared back out at me with large, apprehensive eyes and a sullen mouth, framed by pasta-shaped ringlets of fair hair. She looked as if it hadn't been much fun for her either.

The next day I went to my suburban supermarket, the temple of all my bourgeois consumerist values. There were no worm pills for sale, no top hats, no curry combs, no Barbour-reproofers, no ballgowns, no shotgun cartridges, no kilts, GTi key-rings or packets of Marlboro Lights – nothing to remind me of them. I stood in front of the J-cloths selection for a long while, deliberating as to which I ought to buy. I had to remind myself that I was middle class and that being middle class was the only serious way to be. And then I bought some muesli, just for good measure.